THE AGE
OF IDEOLOGY—
POLITICAL
THOUGHT,
1750
TO THE
PRESENT

PRENTICE-HALL FOUNDATIONS OF MODERN POLITICAL SCIENCE SERIES

Robert A. Dahl, Editor

THE AGE OF IDEOLOGY-POLITICAL THOUGHT, 1750 TO THE PRESENT,
Second Edition
by Isaac Kramnick and Frederick M. Watkins

THE AMERICAN PARTY SYSTEM AND THE AMERICAN PEOPLE,
Second Edition
by Fred I. Greenstein

THE ANALYSIS OF INTERNATIONAL RELATIONS, Second Edition
by Karl W. Deutsch

CONGRESS AND THE PRESIDENCY, Third Edition
by Nelson W. Polsby

DATA ANALYSIS FOR POLITICS AND POLICY
by Edward R. Tufte

MODERN POLITICAL ANALYSIS, Third Edition
by Robert A. Dahl

MODERN POLITICAL ECONOMY
by Norman Frohlich and Joe A. Oppenheimer

NORMATIVE POLITICAL THEORY
by Fred M. Frohock

PERSPECTIVES IN CONSTITUTIONAL LAW, with Revisions
by Charles L. Black, Jr.

THE POLICY-MAKING PROCESS
by Charles E. Lindblom

PUBLIC OPINION
by Robert E. Lane and David O. Sears

PUBLIC ADMINISTRATION (Forthcoming)
by James W. Fesler

PRENTICE-HALL FOUNDATIONS OF MODERN POLITICAL SCIENCE SERIES

Robert A. Dahl, Editor

PRENTICE-HALL, INC., Englewood Cliffs, New Jersey 07632

THE AGE
OF IDEOLOGY–
POLITICAL
THOUGHT,
1750
TO THE
PRESENT

Second Edition

ISAAC KRAMNICK

Cornell University

FREDERICK M. WATKINS

Library of Congress Cataloging in Publication Data

Kramnick, Isaac (date).
　　The Age of Ideology.

　　Prentice-Hall Foundations of Modern Political Science Series
　　First ed. (1964) by F. M. Watkins.
　　Bibliography: p. 103
　　Includes index.
　　1. Political science History. 2. Watkins, Frederick
Mundell (date),　　joint author. II. Title.
JA83.W3　　　1979　　　320.5'09　　　78-16090
ISBN 0-13-018499-3

PRENTICE-HALL FOUNDATIONS OF MODERN POLITICAL SCIENCE SERIES

Robert A. Dahl, Editor

THE AGE OF IDEOLOGY—POLITICAL THOUGHT, 1750 TO THE PRESENT
SECOND EDITION
by Isaac Kramnick and Frederick M. Watkins

PRENTICE-HALL INTERNATIONAL, INC., London

PRENTICE-HALL OF AUSTRALIA, PTY. LTD., Sydney

PRENTICE-HALL OF CANADA, LTD., Toronto

PRENTICE-HALL OF INDIA PRIVATE LIMITED, New Delhi

PRENTICE-HALL OF JAPAN, INC., Tokyo

PRENTICE-HALL OF SOUTHEAST ASIA PTE. LTD., Singapore

WHITEHALL BOOKS LIMITED, WELLINGTON, New Zealand

10 9 8 7 6 5

CONTENTS

S. Bell

PREFACE

Our modern age is preeminently an Age of Ideology. It is true that, in one sense of the term, ideology has always been and always will be with us. There has never been a time when human behavior, including political behavior, has not been largely affected by the mental images, or stereotypes, through which people have grown accustomed to perceive and judge the world around them. One of the books in this series, Lane and Sears, *Public Opinion*, is devoted to that very basic problem. But the ideologies with which we are here concerned are quite a different matter. These ideologies are the broad and comprehensive doctrines—like liberalism, communism, or fascism—which have emerged in the past two hundred years as a peculiar and often decisive factor in contemporary politics. In ways that were never true before, our modern wars are ideological wars, our party conflicts ideological conflicts. Without some understanding of the nature and effects of these ideologies, no study of modern politics, foreign or domestic, could possibly make sense. To provide an introductory basis for coming to grips with this problem is the purpose of this book.

As compared to the various methods used in other volumes of this series, the method we shall be following here is essentially historical. The need for such an approach is implicit in the nature of the material. Although our main concern, as political scientists, is to show how ideologies, here and now, are capable of influencing political behavior, we cannot hope to do so without looking to the past. Beginning with the liberalism that played so great a part in the American and French Revolutions, each ideology has arisen in response to the hopes and needs of a particular time, and has been modified or replaced by others in the light of subsequent experience. The only possible way of understanding why they are as they are today is to begin at the beginning and trace them through their successive stages of development down to the present time. Only thus can we hope to explain the nature and extent of their influence in the world in which we live.

The subject is too vast to be covered at all fully in a book as short as this. We shall therefore be considering the Age of Ideology in terms of a very limited number of writers taken as representative of their respective schools of thought. Any such selection is bound to be somewhat arbitrary and runs the risk of doing less than justice to the material. The best it can hope to do is to lay down some preliminary guidelines that may prove useful as a basis for further study. From the authors' standpoint, the most satisfactory reader of this book will be the one who finds it inadequate, and goes in search of more.

Frederick M. Watkins
Isaac Kramnick

THE AGE
OF IDEOLOGY—
POLITICAL
THOUGHT,
1750
TO THE
PRESENT

CHAPTER ONE

IDEOLOGY AND REVOLUTION

For the past two centuries the Western world has been living through what might well be called the Age of Ideologies. Political life has been an arena where secular ideas and ideals fight it out. With the demise of the religious unity that was medieval Catholic Europe and with the faith in progress spawned by the Enlightenment and The Industrial Revolution has come The Age of Ideology. The crucial political institutions of the modern age, the party and mobilized public opinion, operate in a world where ideas and ideals have become the driving force of politics. It is not only the age-old quest for power and glory that brings men and women into political life, but also burning commitments to clashing visions of ideal order.

IDEOLOGY-THE WORD AND THE CONCEPT

The word *ideology* appeared for the first time late in the eighteenth century. Coined by an obscure French disciple of John Locke, Destutt de Tracy (1754–1836), the word *ideologie* was intended to convey a theory of learning which described the origin of abstract ideas in a mind otherwise formed by sense experiences. Political connotations were added to the word when Napoleon used *ideologues* to malign not only intellectuals like de Tracy but all men of ideas. They were blind to historical reality in their pursuit of abstract truths and they were troublemakers as wielders of ideas in the quest for reform and improvement.

Ideology as a concept has had a tortuous history since the days of de Tracy and Napoleon. What has remained fairly constant has been its association with debate over the role of ideas, especially political ideas, in shaping and determining historical and social development. For some like Mannheim, ideology has meant the "social determination" or the "social-conditioning" of ideas, the origins of thought in group life and social position. For some ideology has meant beliefs, sets of beliefs, or myths, that influence and justify political behavior. For others in the Marxist tradition, for example, ideology is an intellectual superstructure, a secondary realm of ideas built upon the primary foundation, the material substructure of society. Ideology, then, is a false consciousness. The thinker is unaware of the real motive forces that condition his or her thought. This is not unlike the view of another school, associated with Nietzsche and Pareto, which sees ideology as thought or beliefs determined by unknown instinctual and irrational motives.

In this book we do not pursue this lively intellectual debate over the nature and function of ideology. We use the term in its most common colloquial sense as a set of ideas involving visionary and grandiose schemes of social change. Ideologies, for our purposes, are patterns of political beliefs that introduce normative visions into political life. These visions of ideal order usually include highly articulated attitudes about human nature, about the relationship of the individual to the state and society, about the relationship of the economy and the polity, and about the goals and purposes of politics in general. In The Age of Ideologies, then, it is the clash of these visions which is at the center of political life.

THE REVOLUTIONARY CHARACTER
OF MODERN IDEOLOGIES

Since the American and French Revolutions, political ideologies have been based on the revolutionary conviction that life here on earth is capable of being perfected by human knowledge and effort. In most periods of history any such proposition would have been rejected by most people as being absurdly unrealistic. The usual expectation was that people would go on living much as their ancestors had done, experiencing the various joys and privations to which, as it then seemed, flesh was naturally heir. All this has changed in the past 200 years. Revolutionary advances in industry, science and technology have adorned life with telephones and televisions and other hitherto unimaginable amenities, and have gone a long way toward routing man's perennial enemies, disease and starvation. Although many of the more spectacular innovations have been reserved for the twentieth century, many people were able from the beginning to recognize the vast potentialities of the emerging new age. As early even as the eighteenth century, supporters of the American and French Revolutions were already inspired by the exciting vision of wonders soon to come. From that day to this, hopes first aroused and continually nourished by the belief in the inevitability of progress have never ceased to provide successive ideological movements with their primary appeals.

Less obvious, but no less important, is the fact that the Industrial Revolution itself could never have occurred, or never at least in the rapid and comprehensive form it actually assumed, without the aid and support of these selfsame ideological movements. We all know how much communism and, to a lesser extent, nationalism has contributed in our own day to the drastic modernization of many underdeveloped areas. The industrialization of the USSR is the most famous case in point. Because it all took place so long ago, we tend to forget that the industrialization of the Western world was also, in its initial stages, a fairly drastic and highly ideological process. Beginning with the American and French Revolutions, the West experienced a series of revolutionary disturbances which reached their culmination in 1848. These disturbances, under the inspiration of liberal and nationalist ideas, were a forcible and ultimately successful attempt to speed up the process of modernization by overthrowing conservative forces of resistance. The Industrial Revolution itself owes much to the power of ideology.

A typical feature of modern ideologies is their militantly revolutionary character, to be sure. This is a natural, though by no means necessary, consequence of their close relationship to the process of technological innovation. Sanctioned though it is by long usage, the term "Industrial Revolution" is something of a misnomer. Rapid as it may be, the technological transformation of a society is a matter of evolutionary changes rather than of revolutionary leaps. For anyone impatient to enjoy the fruits of innovation, the tempo of such changes may well seem to be unconscionably slow. In politics, on the other hand, revolutionary changes are entirely possible. Whenever anticipated evolutionary improvements fail to take place on schedule, it is quite natural to try to speed up the economic process by political means. The characteristic function of modern ideologies has been to persuade men that it was both possible and right for them to further the progress of the Industrial Revolution by launching a revolutionary attack against the established political order.

The common revolutionary character of modern ideologies goes far to explain a number of other characteristics which they likewise share in common. Revolution is a taxing process which imposes its own laws. People are in large measure creatures of habit. They generally fear and resent the prospect of any profound or extensive changes in their way of life. This is particularly apt to be true of those who, as political or social leaders of the community, already enjoy a comparatively favorable position. The way of the revolutionary, then, has always been a hard one. To compensate their followers for the immediate risks and discomforts of change, they must inspire them with a compelling belief in the value of future rewards. In the process they must also, in most cases, persuade them to break their habitual bonds of allegiance to established political authorities. To overcome people's fear of change, and to justify new forms of allegiance, are the central problems to be solved by any theory of revolution. If modern ideologies all share certain common characteristics, it is because they have all tended, as products of a common revolutionary age, to find common solutions to these two inescapable problems.

IDEOLOGY AND THE MASSES

The revolutionary character of modern ideologies is further revealed by their self-conscious evocation of the people as the ultimate beneficiary of progress and ideological victory. To a greater extent than ever before in history, modern ideological movements have been ultimately popular movements, claiming popular approval as the legitimate basis of authority. Opinions may well differ about the degree of popular support actually enjoyed by any particular government. At the present time, the people's democracies of the East, and the constitutional democracies of the West, each claim that they, and they alone, are genuinely democratic. The heat raised by this controversy is striking evidence of the fact that the importance of being democratic is one point, at least, on which even the most antagonistic ideologues are able to agree.

This state of affairs has continued for so long that it is easy to take it for granted. Until comparatively recent times, however, democracy was not at all a word that brought universal approval. During most of recorded history, divine right and ancient usage have been accepted by the people themselves as the normal grounds of political obligation. The Western world has, until recently, adhered to the common view. Having read in the Bible that the powers that be are ordained by God, Christians have generally been reluctant to disobey political authorities, and have sought to justify rebellion, on the rare occasions when they have thought it justifiable, by showing that the established government has forfeited its claim to allegiance by gross disobedience to the commandments of its proper master, God. Thus the idea that popular consent and participation are the touchstones of political legitimacy is far from commonplace.

For most of Western history, the common assumptions of social life set narrow limits to the possible scope of popular participation in politics. The ancient Greeks believed that popular government was possible only in a state small enough so that the entire citizen body could come together and hear the words of a single orator. This belief was substantially correct, as things stood then and long thereafter. The Industrial Revolution soon led, however, to dramatic and unprecedented increases in the ease and scope of public communication. Growing rates of literacy gave new meaning to the old art of printing, and a series of new inventions, from railroads to television and beyond, provided along with newspapers, still furthered opportunities for maintaining contact with ever larger masses of people. Rapidly changing economic and social conditions aided the process by breaking down many of the class and local differences that had long stood as barriers between people. Under these circumstances, it has become possible, for the first time in history, to articulate and seek to implement broad based revolutionary ideals.

Modern ideologies are the first attempts to cope with this novel environment. As distinguished from the political thought of earlier times, they are grandiose and visionary schemes for restructuring the political world that have been designed in light of the unprecedented problems and opportunities posed by an age of growing mass participation in politics.

THREE CHARACTERISTIC FEATURES
OF MODERN IDEOLOGY

There are, in addition to their revolutionary and popular character, certain other special traits which are characteristic and distinctive features of modern ideologies. In the first place, the goals to which modern ideologies address themselves are typically utopian and apocalyptic. It is much easier to keep up your courage when there is a prospect of decisive victory, a victory that involves the establishment of a new and ideal order. Modern ideologists normally tend, therefore, to define their goals in decisive and optimistic terms. The liberal concept of the free market, or the Marxist concept of the classless society, are typical of this utopian trend. In each case the assumption is that once the promised goal has been reached other taxing problems of modern life will promptly disappear.

A second characteristic of modern ideologists is their habit of thinking in the simplified terms of "we" and "they," of friend and enemy. This is, indeed, a natural corollary and symptom of their basic utopianism. People who believe that their goals are absolutely overwhelmingly in the public interest will suspect something sinister about the motives of those who reject their conclusions. Surely those who persist in refusing so great a good must be bad, or at least invincibly ignorant. This line of reasoning encourages the more ardent ideologists to disregard intermediate shades of opinion and to look on political differences as a matter of black and white. They and their associates are fighting for the interests of all mankind, while their opponents are selfishly or ignorantly supporting minority interests at the expense of the general good. Free people versus tyrants, middle class versus aristocracy, the racially pure versus the racially defiled, proletarians versus capitalists, patriots versus imperialists —such clear-cut alternatives are typical of the ideological way of seeing political realities. This point of view has contributed greatly to the vigor and self-confidence of all modern ideological movements.

A third and final characterisitic of modern ideologies is also worth keeping in mind, though it is not quite so general as the two already mentioned. Until the end of the nineteenth century, and to some extent even now, successful ideological movements have derived much of their strength from the extreme optimism of their views regarding human progress. One of the significant features of the Industrial Revolution was that it has generally seemed to encourage the prospects of radical innovation. In an age of rapidly increasing technological progress, it was easy to conclude that the progressive improvement of human welfare was an inevitable function of time itself, and was bound to continue in the future. If progress is the law of history, it follows that the "wave of the future" is on the side of the friends, and against the enemies, of human welfare. Since the supporters of modern ideologies regularly believe that they alone are on the side of progress, the result has been to give them confidence in the ultimate victory as well as in the justice of their cause.

IDEOLOGY AND HISTORICAL CHANGE

Modern science and technology, productive as they may have been in terms of human welfare, have not only solved but also raised hard problems. Thus the Age of Ideologies has been an age both of high hopes and of dark disillusionments. Utopian vision has followed utopian vision, each destined to grow dim in its turn. Ideologically, as in so many other ways, the modern world has proved to be in constant flux.

The ideological aspect of modern politics is the subject of this book. Although its primary interest is in present-day problems, its method of approach will be essentially historical. All the main ideologies of the past 200 years are still very much alive. Liberalism, nationalism, and Marxism first rose to prominence in the eighteenth and nineteenth centuries, and all are vital factors in the contemporary world. But even though they remain alive, ideologies are constantly changing. When old utopian hopes are disappointed, they must either be revised or replaced by new ones. To unravel the ideological forces operative at any given time and place is a highly complex matter. New ideologies compete with older ideologies in various stages of revision. Ideological excesses may also encourage the growth of anti-ideologies, like Burkean conservatism in the late eighteenth century or American neo-conservatism in the 1970s which urge the rejection of utopianism in any shape or form. The only way to comprehend the nature and direction of all these various movements is to see how each in turn has grown out of and reacted against the others. Contemporary ideologies are the outcome of a course of development that runs all the way from the American Revolution down to the present day. To follow that course of development is the plan of the present study.

CHAPTER TWO

LIBERALISM I: THE AMERICAN REVOLUTION

Read Declaration

The year 1776 is notable for two separate but closely related events: in America the signing of the Declaration of Independence, and in Britain the publication of Adam Smith's *The Wealth of Nations.* Smith was one of the earliest representatives of what soon came to be known as the classical school of laissez-faire economics. His book, an eloquent demonstration of the advantages of international free trade, was the first great manifesto of economic liberalism. Although this work appeared too late to have any direct influence on the signers of the Declaration, the fact that the two documents appeared within a few months of each other was no mere coincidence. Both were the outgrowth of common currents of thought and feeling that had long been circulating on both sides of the Atlantic and derived from the writings of the late seventeenth century prophet of liberal ideology, John Locke. *The Wealth of Nations,* by reflecting the liberal climate of opinion in terms of a clear and impressive theory, marked the coming of age of the earliest of our modern ideologies. The Declaration of Independence reflected that same climate of opinion, in part at least, in its call to rebellion, thus inaugurating the first of a long line of modern revolutionary movements. Thus these two events in 1776, far from being unrelated, reinforced each other. Between them they gave that year a real claim to the distinction of being the Year One of the Age of Ideology.

THE LIBERALISM OF JOHN LOCKE

The dominant political ideals shared by both sides of the Atlantic in the late eighteenth century were derived from Locke's *Second Treatise of Civil Government* (1679–81). His ideas were reflected in the editorials of the Philadelphia press, the sermons of Boston pulpits, and the writings of such British economic Liberals as Adam Smith. Locke argued that individuals voluntarily created governments through contractual agreements. People consented to be governed because governments were needed to protect the natural rights of individuals to life, liberty, and property. If governments failed to protect these sacred natural rights, the people, Locke argued, could legitimately change their government. They had not agreed to be governed by tyrants who threatened their freedom or property, but by neutral governors who in fact secured and defended these basic rights.

Locke's arguments were revolutionary. He denied that people were born into given governmental arrangements in which an obligation to obey their governors was dictated by God, by divine right, by aristocratic or hereditary customs and traditions. Government, Locke insisted, derived its legitimacy from the consent of the governed, who had agreed to obey government in a contractual decision which was voluntary and rational. Free, equal, and independent people agreed to be governed in return for the certain and secure enjoyment of their individual rights which the courts and police powers of a government enforced. Government was legitimate, then, as long as people continued to consent to it. Locke assumed this would be the case as long as the government in turn protected the economic and human rights of its citizens. The revolutionary impact of these liberal ideas is clearly reflected in the Declaration of Independence, whose language Jefferson actually borrowed from the writings of Locke.

A second revolutionary aspect of Locke's liberalism is its focus on individuals, on their self-interest and property rights. Freedom for Locke becomes the passive enjoyment of personal and individual rights. Individuals have a moral right to be protected from the interference by governments or other individuals of their sacred rights to life, liberty, and private property. Earlier social and political writings had tended to absorb individuals in larger corporate entities—family, church, community, or profession—and to subordinate their personal interests to the interests of these larger social bodies. Liberalism in Locke's writings envisions a social order of autonomous and independent individuals who are responsible for their own fate and who seek their own personal interest. The revolutionary dimension of this liberal ideal would also reveal itself in Smith's *Wealth of Nations*.

9

THE ECONOMIC THEORIES
OF ADAM SMITH

Adam Smith was concerned with the product of a new relationship between government and business that was growing increasingly prevalent in the eighteenth century. To provide for the economic welfare of their subjects has normally been reckoned as one of the primary responsibilities of good rulers. The traditional method of doing this had been for the government itself, in very large measure, to direct and control the economy. This meant looking after the poor, as well as regulating the market. In the earlier stages of the Industrial Revolution enlightened rulers played a leading part in economic development. By granting patents of monopoly and other special privileges, ambitious princes vied with one another in encouraging the development of commerce and industry in their respective realms. The over-all policy, a policy generally known as mercantilism, sought to maintain a favorable balance of international trade, to encourage exports and discourage imports. All this was, in many ways, quite favorable to innovation. In their attempt to capture foreign markets, and at the same time to find domestic substitutes for costly foreign imports, mercantilist governments were much interested in the improvement of commercial and industrial methods. But as time went on, mercantilism came increasingly to be regarded more as a hindrance than as a help to economic progress. Merchants and manufacturers, in proportion as they gained in wealth and experience, became less dependent on legal privileges, more impatient of legal restraints. Industrialists who feel that their goods are the equal of any will be indifferent to tariff protection and resentful of tariff restrictions. Under these circumstances, government regulation is seen as a bane, not a blessing, thus calling into question traditional views of the relationship between economics and politics.

The purpose of *The Wealth of Nations* was to demonstrate that true economic welfare is to be achieved not by mercantilist or by any other methods of regulating world trade, but by freeing it completely from restriction and control. The real wealth of individuals and communities is not measured by the possession of greater or lesser quantities of gold and silver; what matters is the quantity and quality of goods and services at their disposal. If the more efficient producers are free to sell wherever they wish, competition between them will automatically bring prices down to a uniform level, to a world market price, and consumers will get more and better goods for their money. If this process is interfered with in any way, better goods will be driven off the market, thus forcing consumers to buy the shoddier and costlier products of less efficient producers. Thus the simple and natural law of supply and demand, when allowed to follow its own course, automatically maximizes economic welfare; and any government that interferes with this spontaneous process is merely decreasing the wealth of nations.

IDEOLOGICAL IMPLICATIONS
OF LAISSEZ-FAIRE ECONOMICS

Although Adam Smith went less far than some of his successors in praise of the free market, his economic liberalism already included the raw materials for an effective ideology. His argument for international free trade is merely a special case of the more general proposition that individual self-interest is the primary instrument of social progress. Since, as the argument runs, men and women are the best judges of their own particular needs and capacities, it follows that the most rational use of human and material resources will occur automatically if people are allowed to follow their natural bent under conditions of free competition. This is true not only in international trade but in general everywhere. If people are forcibly prevented from doing as they wish, their natural inventiveness and enterprise will be stifled; if these innovative forces are liberated, there is bound to be a rapid and progressive improvement in the conditions of human existence. In the light of hindsight, it is easy to see that these hopes, though not wholly unfounded, were much exaggerated. The picture of a perfectly free market, entirely dominated by motives of rational self-interest, is clearly a utopian oversimplification of the world as it really does or could exist. At a time, however, when the Industrial Revolution was actually opening up unprecedented opportunities for industrial innovation, the promise of a progressive and automatically self-regulating economy was both attractive and exciting. Smith's economic ideal of a naturally harmonious social order, when joined to Locke's political vision, would form the theoretical foundation of liberal ideology.

IDEOLOGICAL ASPECTS
OF THE AMERICAN REVOLUTION

Something more was needed, however, to translate the economic theories of Smith and the political theories of Locke into an effective ideological movement, which brings us to the importance of the American Revolution. This is not to say that the American revolutionists self-consciously sought the achievement of a liberal utopia. To a very large extent, indeed, the colonists in North America regarded themselves as heirs to the traditional rights of the English. When relationships with the home country deteriorated, therefore, it was natural for the revolutionists to justify themselves as defenders of the established constitution. This essentially conservative line of thought never ceased to play an important part in the American Revolution. But the supporters of the movement also included a much more radical wing. Emphasizing natural rather than traditional rights, they tended to look not backwards but forwards, to the establishment of new liberties. Their efforts lent a strongly, though never exclusively, ideological aspect to the American Revolution.

Hostility to mercantilism was the factor that probably did the most to move the American colonists in the direction of liberalism. The nature of mercantilism was such that colonial dependencies were bound to become peculiarly aware of its disadvantages. According to mercantilist theory, the special function of colonies was to produce a favorable balance of international trade by supplying the home country with raw materials that otherwise would have to be bought abroad, and by providing it with a protected market for its manufactured goods. This was the objective of the Navigation Acts and the other measures proposed first by Grenville and then Townshend, that regulated the economic relations between Great Britain and America. The colonists were generally required to confine their trade to British markets, and their attempts to set up industrial establishments were severely limited. In a new land with limitless opportunities for economic enterprise, these restrictions soon became a grievance. Since free trade had never been one of the traditional rights of the English, a conservative defense of those rights could hardly justify any thoroughgoing assertion of American economic interest. Revolutionary liberalism was bound under such circumstances to exert a strong appeal.

In 1775 the state of affairs was still in a state of flux. Overt hostilities had already broken out; this was the year of Concord and Lexington. Through the Sons of Liberty and the Committees of Correspondence, the extremists had already succeeded in laying the organizational foundations for a popular revolutionary movement. But the die was not yet cast. The ties of traditional loyalty were still strongly felt, and there had been as yet no Declaration of Independence to commit the colonists irrevocably to the breaking of those ties. Many believed that, if adequate concessions were made to the American position on questions of taxation without representation and other such matters, all might yet be well. On the British side there were also those who favored a course of compromise and adjustment. This point of view had already been strongly expressed in Edmund Burke's famous speech on the conciliation of the American colonies. Which way the course of events would turn was far from being certain.

PAINE'S *COMMON SENSE*

At this point a new factor was introduced into the situation—the third great document of 1776, Thomas Paine's *Common Sense.* This revolutionary pamphlet quickly gained a circulation, and exerted an influence, that mark it as one of the most successful documents in the whole long history of political polemics. The author was not an American but a thirty-seven-year-old immigrant fresh from England. His experiences as a poor and unsuccessfully enterprising member of a still largely traditional and caste-bound society had made him a radical democrat and libertarian. To him, as to many another immigrant before and since, America was the land of opportunity, the country where persons could hope to escape the bonds of hereditary privilege and vested interests, and to make the most of their own abilities in an atmosphere of social and political freedom. Liberalism was his religion, the New World his promised land. Unlike most Americans, he believed that the approaching revolution ought to be a struggle not for the traditional liberties of the English, but for the revolutionary rights of man. His state of mind, in other words, was essentially ideological. His purpose in writing *Common Sense* was to persuade the American people to make a decisive break with their British past and commit themselves to a future of democratic liberalism. To a greater extent than anyone else, he represented and encouraged the ideological aspects of the American Revolution.

THE LIBERAL THEORY OF GOVERNMENT

The central doctrine of Paine's liberalism, as of liberalism in general, is a belief in the possibilities of spontaneous social action and a corresponding minimization of the need for government. Like the vast majority of liberals, he did not go so far as to adopt a purely anarchist position. He recognized that human nature is less than perfect, and that people, if left to their own devices, would often use their liberty to impair the liberty of others. Coercion, after all, is equally destructive of freedom no matter whether it is applied by private individuals or by official tyrants. Government is a necessary and proper device to safeguard the person and property of free persons. Most of the positive values of human life, including economic values, are a result of spontaneous social action; the primary function of government is not to create values of its own, but to prevent criminals from impairing the values created by society. In short, Paine believed that government is a necessary evil. To keep that evil down to the irreducible minimum was nothing more or less, to his way of thinking, than an elementary dictate of common sense.

13

THE PROBLEM
OF POLITICAL OPPRESSION

Paine clearly thinks that his criterion of good government is a revolutionary innovation, and that few if any governments, past or present, have
ever come within reasonable distance of satisfying its requirements. But
if the liberal conception of politics and government is just a matter of
common sense, how then does it happen that liberalism has not long
since been a matter of common practice? What possibly could have prevented people, as rational beings, from adopting so rational a solution to
the problem of politics?

Paine answers this problem by insisting that, though people are
reasonable creatures, they can also be deceived. By exploiting the gulli-
bility of the masses, and more especially by playing on their superstitious
fears, ambitious individuals from the earliest times have regularly succeeded in persuading them to accept irrational and repressive forms of
government. The most common, and nonsensical of these forms of government is hereditary monarchy. Since the possession of political power
enables the ruling classes to enjoy special privileges at the expense of
their fellow citizens, it is obviously in their own self-interest to maintain
and extend the coercive powers of government. They, and they alone, are
the forces that have always stood, and still stand, as obstacles to the
freedom and happiness of mankind.

The objectives and the enemies of liberalism once identified, the
correct program of action follows as a simple matter of course. Since the
ruling classes are committed to the maintenance of an oppressive *status
quo,* their enmity to liberal governments is a matter of direct personal
interest. The consequence is that, from a liberal standpoint, the proper
policy must be to encourage the people to rebel against their existing
rulers and assume the responsibilities of government.

THE NEED FOR REVOLUTION

In *Common Sense,* Paine applied these general principles to the specific
issues of the American Revolution. British government was doing much
more than its limited mandate allowed. In fact, far from protecting the
individual rights of American colonists, this oppressive tyrant threatened
them. It was necessary, however, to persuade the colonists to make a final
break with Great Britain. Recognizing that respect for the British Constitution had old and tenacious roots, Paine applied himself particularly to
the task of challenging that tradition. People had long been taught that
the British political system, with its complex balance of powers between
king and Parliament, was the most liberal of all systems, and that to be

a free-born English citizen was to be the freest of all. In reply Paine tried to demonstrate that this freedom was a fraud. Simplicity, he said, is the hallmark of any truly rational system. Thus the complexity of the British Constitution is in itself a sign that something is amiss. With its hereditary king and House of Lords, and its unrepresentative House of Commons, the system is hopelessly undemocratic. In the actual balance of powers, moreover, the king is the decisive force. Hereditary privilege is thus the prevailing feature of the British Constitution. For the American colonists to retain any sort of connection with Great Britain would be to subject themselves to a continuing servitude. Complete independence alone can offer them the blessings of good government and enable them to exchange the illusory rights of the English for the genuine rights of all.

Paine also tried to awaken in the American colonists the sense of being a chosen people, with a special destiny and responsibility of their own. In so doing he hoped to make them share in his own conviction that the triumph of liberalism was not only desirable but also certain. Once an outpost of religious liberty, the new continent was now destined to serve humanity as the model and exemplar of a wholly free society. Unspoiled by ancient evils and corruptions, the New World was uniquely qualified to lead the old toward universal freedom. In fighting for their own liberties, therefore, the colonists would also be fighting for the liberties of all.

THE REVOLUTION
AND LIBERAL IDEOLOGY

Read the Decl. of Indep.

It would be a mistake to think of Paine as the most influential voice of the American Revolution. *Common Sense* undoubtedly influenced the wavering minds of many of its readers and did much to strengthen the current of opinion that led in the course of that same summer to the Declaration of Independence. The Declaration was itself, however, less a monument to Paine than one to John Locke. When Jefferson chose to justify the break with Britain, he used the ideas of *The Second Treatise of Civil Government.* Men were created with certain natural and inalienable rights, the most important being life, liberty, and the pursuit of happiness. To protect these rights men had set up governments whose authority rested on their consent. When a government ceased to do what it had been set up for, its citizens had a right to change it in order to once again provide for their safety and happiness. The cause of the Americans was wrapped in the general theory of liberalism.

Not all Americans in 1776 shared the liberal theory of revolution contained in the *Declaration,* let alone Paine's ideological fervor. From first to last, the radical aspects of the movement were balanced by a strand of persistent conservatism. Its leaders were mostly men with a good deal of practical experience in political matters. Many of them had, to say the least, a less than utopian confidence in the spontaneous wisdom and goodness of the masses. They also had a good deal of respect for traditional institutions and procedures. Their influence did much to moderate revolutionary hopes.

And yet, to a very large extent, Paine's highest hopes were vindicated. The American Revolution succeeded not only in breaking the ties with Great Britain but also in creating a new nation peculiarly committed to new principles. When the Great Seal of the United States was adopted, the motto chosen for its reverse side was *Novus ordo seclorum,* a new order of the ages. Thus was expressed the conviction, a belief shared by many foreigners as well as by most Americans, that the establishment of the United States marked an epoch in world history, the dawning of a new and better age of democratic freedom.

CHAPTER THREE

LIBERALISM II: THE FRENCH REVOLUTION

Few people have ever managed to play an active and significant part in two major revolutions. That most unusual privilege was reserved for Thomas Paine. It was remarkable enough that an Englishman should have turned up in America just in time to become an outstanding figure in the American Revolution. It is still more remarkable to find this same man in Paris, some twenty years later, serving as a member of the National Assembly, which accomplished an even greater revolution in the affairs of France. In his second revolutionary venture he was, to be sure, less influential than in the first. No word or deed of his had any appreciable impact on French opinion, and by voting against the execution of Louis XVI he even found himself in jail for a while. Nevertheless, he was and remained an ardent supporter of the new revolutionary movement. And his pamphleteering skill enabled him, at an early stage of proceedings, to produce a work, *The Rights of Man*, that immediately gained recognition in the English-speaking world as the ablest and most effective defense of the revolutionary position.

Paine regarded the two revolutions as closely related episodes in a common movement toward the liberation of humanity. His opinion was essentially correct. Both were, to a very large extent, expressions of a common ideology, and their joint example did much to encourage the dissemination of that ideology throughout the Western world. When the French Republic, in 1885, presented the American people with the colossal statue of Liberty now standing in New York harbor, it paid grateful tribute to the common bond uniting the two nations.

THE FRENCH AND AMERICAN
REVOLUTIONS COMPARED

When the French and American revolutions are closely examined, how-ever, it becomes apparent that there are important differences, as well as likenesses, between the two movements. In America the liberal tradition soon came to be the common sense of the people, a bond of union joining them in a common national purpose; in France the revolution still re-mains, after nearly 200 years, a controversial issue. French politics, and European politics in general, are marked to this day by ideological cleav-ages that are much more pervasive than in the American experience. These differences stem from the distinctive character of European liber-alism, as it emerged from the French Revolution.

If liberal ideas took hold in America with relative ease, it was be-cause social conditions had always been much freer there than on the continent of Europe. When the English settlers first arrived in the New World, they brought with them many of the traditional class distinctions of the old country. These distinctions did not disappear quickly or com-pletely. Down to the end of the colonial period, for example, the author-ities at Harvard and Yale had to face the annual headache of listing the incoming class not by alphabetical but by social precedence. With the exceptions of slavery and the all-pervasive subordination of women, legal and customary restrictions on social mobility were comparatively mild, which meant that the break with Great Britain could be accomplished without any very drastic changes in the established social order. Eu-ropean society, on the contrary, was a complex network of long-estab-lished privileges and distinctions. The vocations that persons might follow, the taxes they had to pay, even the religion they might profess, were largely determined by the accident of birth, differing widely from class to class and from region to region. The liberal idea of free competi-tion and of equal rights for all was radically at variance with the existing way of life. Under these circumstances, far more than in America, liberal-ism was bound to appear as a thoroughgoing social revolution.

THE REVOLUTIONARY FERMENT
IN EIGHTEENTH-CENTURY FRANCE

France was the country where discontent with the established order first came to a head. In the eighteenth century the French were the intellectual and cultural leaders of the world, chief exponents of the new current of thought, known as the Enlightenment, that marked the coming of the scientific and industrial revolutions. But France was also, in many ways, a country peculiarly resistant to innovation. Traditional monopolies and other vested interests stood in the way of economic progress. Legal barriers and restrictions inhibited social mobility, and official censorship by both the monarchy and the church stood as a constant, if rather ineffective, threat to the free exchange of ideas. The great and increasing privileges of the nobility, including their virtual exemption from taxation, aroused particular resentment at a time when the nation, partly as a consequence of expenses incurred in support of the American Revolution, was rapidly approaching bankruptcy. Of all the countries of Europe, France was the one, therefore, where progressive and liberal ideas came most sharply into conflict with the existing political and social realities. A highly explosive situation was quite clearly in the making.

At the time when Paine wrote his *Common Sense,* influential French people were already fully acquainted with and sympathetic to the theory of liberalism. The philosophical principles of the Enlightenment had given them faith in a happier and more progressive world that would follow automatically upon the liberation of individuals from undue political restrictions. They also believed that time was inevitably on the side of progress, and that the selfish vested interests now standing in its way would lose out in the long run. What they still lacked was any sort of confidence in the possibility of using democratic means for the attainment of liberal purposes. In America Paine had already recommended that the people should stop appealing to the king and take power into their own hands. This was feasible because the colonists had long had representative institutions of their own and were in a position to use existing colonial legislatures, and experienced political leaders, as agencies of revolutionary action. In France there were no comparable agencies. Under its absolute monarchy the only established channel for the redressing of grievances was an appeal to the king himself. This long remained the only hope of the liberal-minded French.

THE REVOLUTIONARY CRISIS

In 1789 affairs took a new and revolutionary turn with the election of the Estates General. Bankruptcy had finally forced the king to revive this ancient legislative body, last convened in 1611, in a belated effort to retrieve the situation. Although by this time there was a widespread desire for liberal reforms, the Estates as originally constituted were a most unpromising means of achieving them. They consisted of three separate chambers elected respectively by the clergy, the nobility, and the rest of the population, and the agreement of all three was required for any sort of authoritative action. In view of the prevailing discontent, it was clear from the beginning that radical reformers would win the Third Estate by a large majority. In the other two, however, they could hardly hope for more than a minority position. The nobility and the clergy were the classes, after all, whose privileges were most directly threatened by the rise of liberalism; and even though there were many liberals among them, it was unlikely that either group as a whole would go far in that direction. Thus the only way to make the Estates General serve reformist purposes was to change their essential character. The radical reformers of the Third Estate managed to do just that. By a series of maneuvers, they first arranged to double the size of the popular chamber, and then insisted that all three chambers be merged in a unified National Assembly. The result was to give the French revolutionists, at last, an advantage enjoyed from the beginning by their American predecessors. Secure in their control of a national assembly, they could now if necessary defy the king and proceed in the name of the people. The stage had been set for a second experiment in revolutionary democracy.

The result was the first great triumph of modern ideology, a triumph which, in its revolutionary consequences, makes the American Revolution seem comparatively tame. As voices for the Third Estate, the revolutionists claimed that they and they alone were genuine representatives of the nation. The progressive philosophy of the Enlightenment gave them confidence in their mission. Believing that the progressive realization of universal welfare and happiness was the predestined outcome of history and that individual freedom was the necessary and sufficient means to the attainment of that end, the revolutionists felt that theirs was the cause of reason itself. In the National Assembly they passed by acclamation a *Declaration of the Rights of Man*, which outlawed at a single stroke the whole complex structure of special privileges and guaranteed the principle of equal rights for all. This was soon followed by a complete reorganization of local government, by the adoption of a decimal system of weights and measures, and even by the introduction of a new, and short-lived, Revolutionary calendar. Few countries have ever adopted so many drastic changes in so short a time. Here, for the first time in history, the revolutionary force of liberal democracy was demonstrated to the full.

FIGARO AND THE IDEOLOGY
OF THE REVOLUTION

As the National Assembly went about transforming French social, economic, and political life in the early 1790s, it was motivated by ideals central to liberal ideology. The elimination of feudal obligations and duties, the ending of primogeniture, the proclamation of the rights of property, all speak to the primacy in the political system of free individuals. The revolutionaries in their quest for liberty, fraternity, and equality were not, however, levellers. They attacked the aristocracy, but they were not demanding equality of conditions. They articulated a theory of equality basic to liberal ideology, the notion of equality of opportunity. What bothered the revolutionaries were the advantages of privilege and rank that gave to the aristocracy and monarchists the control of government and all desirable social positions. Benefits, power, and position, the revolutionaries insisted, should go to those whose talent, industry, and hard work merited reward. Equality meant fair competition in which no group or person had built-in advantages.

Equal opportunity undermined the fundamental assumption of an aristocratic age. If life was a race for preferment and advantage, liberal theorists of equal opportunity insisted the race be run fairly with everyone having an equal chance to win. The liberal spokesmen for the middle class assumed that in a fair race virtuous self-made individuals of talent and merit would win, not the idle and useless aristocracy.

This liberal ideal of equal opportunity and of careers open to talent was best captured during these revolutionary years in Beaumarchais' famous characterization of Figaro, the barber in his *Barber of Seville* and *Marriage of Figaro*. Beaumarchais was himself a partisan of liberal causes and, in 1784, he created a political stir when he articulated the spirit of revolutionary liberalism in his portrayal of the self-made hero, Figaro, who lectures the Count Almaviva: "Just because you're a great lord, you think you're a genius. Nobility, fortune, rank, position—you're so proud of these things. What have you done to deserve so many rewards? You went to the trouble of being born, and no more." Figaro spoke for his age and its new ideological commitment to equality of opportunity.

THE BREAKDOWN OF CONSENSUS

For all its many accomplishments, however, the French Revolution also revealed a crucial problem, one that has proved to be characteristic of ideological movements in general. The difficulty had to do with the maintenance of consensus.

In America, where the ideological aspect of the Revolution was comparatively weak, this difficulty had not proved to be fatal. Although the movement was at first rejected by a strong loyalist group, its opposition left no lasting scars on the new republic. The break with Great Britain was a shock, no doubt, but it did not involve a complete repudiation of the past. In their colonial legislatures and other organs of local government, the colonists had well-established representative institutions and had developed respected leaders. These institutions enjoyed a measure of popular acceptance, and these leaders had resources of skill and experience that enabled them to effect the transition to a new order without losing the support of the public. In this they were aided by the fact that the objectives of the Revolution were comparatively moderate, calling for no very drastic changes in the social and economic customs of the community. This made it relatively easy for the revolutionary settlement to gain general acceptance.

The French Revolution, on the other hand, enjoyed no similar advantages. Absolute monarchy had given the French people and their leaders little experience, even at the local level, with the problems of government. The Estates General, which had never previously met within living memory, was totally new, both to the country at large and to its own members. When it tried, in the unprecedented guise of a sovereign national assembly, to lead the country through the painful process of total revolution, it soon lost contact with public opinion. Rather than abandon its ideological hopes, the declining radical minority in the Third Estate was forced to keep itself in power by increasingly coercive means.

THE RELIGIOUS ISSUE

The dangerously divisive effect of the French Revolution is well illustrated by the special case of the relations that soon developed between it and the Roman Catholic Church. The traditional position of most Christian churches, Protestant and Catholic alike, had always been that the state has a positive duty to support the true faith, and to aid the church in its proper work of suppressing heresy. Because of its commitment to freedom of speech and religious toleration, liberalism is incompatible with this particular aspect of Christianity.

Even in America the revolutionists were generally liberal-minded enough to insist on the separation of church and state, thereby incurring the hostility of many supporters of the formerly established churches. Religious freedom had long been widely practiced, however, and most Americans, including all of the very large number who belonged to dissenting churches, welcomed disestablishment. Thus the separation of church and state was a principle on which most Americans soon were able to agree. In France the situation was quite different. Roman Catholicism had long been established there as the only legitimate religion, and church institutions were an integral part of the old political order. Disestablishment, and the abolition of clerical privileges, were among the prime objectives of the revolutionary movement. The confiscation of church property soon followed. When these moves met opposition, the revolutionists went still further, and tried to set up a state church of their own. By an act known as the Civil Constitution of the Clergy, the exercise of clerical functions was legally restricted to priests who would swear allegiance to the Revolution rather than to Rome. This had the unfortunate effect of turning liberalism and Christianity into rival doctrines, and of forcing the French to choose between them. Although religion had been a declining force before the Revolution, many still were strong enough in their faith to opt for Christianity. The resulting conflict between clericals and anticlericals has remained from that day to this as one of the most divisive factors in French politics.

ROUSSEAU AND ROBESPIERRE: DEMOCRACY AND DICTATORSHIP

Even more serious in its political consequences was a difference of opinion that emerged not between the Revolution and its enemies, but among the revolutionists themselves. The delegates of the Third Estate were elected by a large majority of the French people, and in the earlier stages of the Revolution they undoubtedly reflected the prevailing state of public opinion. Their representative position became ever more doubtful, however, as the growing radicalism of their measures began to alienate the general public. Many wanted to abide by the increasingly moderate views of their constituents; others, more fanatical in their commitment to the liberal ideology, were so sure they represented the true interests, and therefore the true will, of the people that they were determined to go forward and repress all opposition.

Another issue that divided the revolutionaries was the extent to which the revolutionary government was to be truly democratic. Was the suffrage, for example, to be extended only to large property owners, to all property owners, or to all adult males? The revolutionary liberals became suspicious of universal suffrage when the Jacobin Party spoke for radical democracy, insisting that governing power should be in the hands of all the people. The radical democrats made extensive use of the writings of Jean Jacques Rousseau, author of *The Social Contract* (1762). Rousseau's book proclaimed the only moral political system to be one in which the community and its people were sovereign. Only when the people made their own laws, he wrote, would they be truly free. Only when the common good of the whole community was sought, not particular interests within it, would there be true democracy. Radical democracy was Rousseau's solution. If all the people wrote the law, the likelihood of the common good being served was substantially enhanced.

One of the revolutionary leaders who took Rousseau's writings seriously was Robespierre. He, like Rousseau, saw the best political system as characterized by democracy, equality, and the overriding importance of the common good. One way to insure the preference for the public interest over particular interest, according to Robespierre, was to encourage the love of country. Ordinary and equal citizens who loved their country were thus the backbone of a real democracy. But what if the people did not prefer the community's good to their own? Rousseau had suggested earlier that in such a situation a single legislator was needed to point out to the democratic masses the real interest of the community. Robespierre revived Rousseau's ideas quite literally. Faced with a citizenry not yet used to democratic self-government, Robespierre proclaimed his twelve man Committee of Public Safety to be the voice of the people. Radical democracy, he argued, needed a first stage of tutelage by an enlightened vanguard who knew the sovereign people's true interest. Although this early experiment in party dictatorship would be shortlived, the successors of the Jacobins, down to and including the Emperor Napoleon, were likewise revolutionary extremists who maintained their positions by non-representative means.

THE INTERNATIONAL REVOLUTION

Domestic problems were not, however, the only cause of this development; international pressures also were largely responsible for forcing the revolutionary movement along the road to dictatorship. Even in the case of firmly established constitutional governments, a resort to dictatorial measures often occurs in times of serious military crisis. It was therefore peculiarly unfortunate that the new and untried French Republic found itself involved from the very beginning in a desperate military struggle with practically all of its neighbors. This is, indeed, one of the most striking differences between the American and French revolutions. Although the American colonists had to fight a war against the British, their difficulties were greatly eased by the fact that the rest of the world offered them the advantages of benevolent neutrality, and even of active assistance. The Bourbon monarchies of France and Spain, in particular, welcomed the American Revolution as an opportunity to weaken the rival power of Great Britain. Their intervention brought the war to a successful conclusion and gave the Americans a generation of uninterrupted peace in which to consolidate their constitutional experiments. In the case of France, however, it was the revolutionists, not their enemies, who were diplomatically isolated. Although the first impulse of the neighboring monarchs, as in the earlier revolutionary crisis, was to profit by the discomfiture of an overly powerful rival, they soon took fright at the subversive implications of the revolutionary movement. The execution of the king and queen of France in 1793 was especially alarming and speeded up the movement toward military intervention by the reactionary monarchs of Europe against the revolutionists. As the French Revolution proceeded, therefore, its supporters had to face the grim prospect of fighting, alone and unaided, two simultaneous wars—a civil war against disaffected elements at home and a foreign war against the united powers of Europe. This double crisis did much to encourage and justify the Jacobins in their assumption of dictatorial powers. It also committed the French to a policy of endless foreign warfare, first defensive, then aggressive, that culminated in the military dictatorship of Napoleon.

ACHIEVEMENTS AND LIMITATIONS
OF THE FRENCH REVOLUTION

The ensuing conquest of practically all Europe was the first decisive demonstration of the power of modern ideology. Confident of their mission as crusaders for the liberation of humanity, the revolutionary leaders proceeded with unprecedented energy and determination to wipe out all domestic opposition, and to convert the whole French people into an effective fighting force. Against the small professional armies of their enemies they threw the irresistible weight of the first modern democratic armies, based on universal conscription. These armies were an incomparable military instrument, but they were also more than that; wherever they went, they carried with them the message and promise of the French Revolution. Through their intervention, sweeping liberal reforms were effected in most of Western Europe, parts of which were directly incorporated in the French Empire, while others were placed under the control of tributary governments. Liberal-minded elements in the conquered territories welcomed these developments, especially at first, and lent their aid to the forces of occupation. The result was a wholesale sweeping away of traditional restrictions and a massive liberalization of the political institutions of modern Europe. No subsequent reaction would ever wholly succeed in undoing these accomplishments.

But if the triumph of French arms bore witness to the power of liberalism, the ephemeral quality of their victory also demonstrated its inability to provide a lasting solution to the problems of modern politics. People everywhere were attracted initially by the promise and achievements of liberalism. The revolutionary principle of equal rights for all, by releasing creative energies from the frustrations of an outworn political and social system, seemed on first acquaintance to be about to remove all barriers to progress. However, the speed and extent of the ensuing changes soon led, in the occupied territories no less than in France itself, to unexpectedly disruptive and painful consequences, and thus to increasing alienation. Some of the advantages of innovation were swallowed up, moreover, by the exactions of an aggressive military dictatorship whose war needs called for endless sacrifices of men and money. Pride in the glory of their matchless victories might give the

French some compensation for these sacrifices; not so for the conquered peoples newly impressed into the French imperial system. As their hostility increased, the imperial regime became more oppressive, until it finally collapsed. Abroad as at home, revolutionary liberalism had failed to create an effective political consensus, and dictatorship had proved to be a most inadequate substitute. Such was the outcome of the first great experiment in modern ideology.

CHAPTER FOUR

CONSERVATISM

The defeat of Napoleon at Waterloo, in 1815, marks the end of a major phase in the history of modern ideology. The Emperor went into exile, and Europe returned for a whole generation to the rule of conservative monarchs. This reversal of fortunes was not only a result of the internal weaknesses and final collapse of the revolutionary movement but was also the outcome of a new and increasingly powerful body of anti-revolutionary thought. Conservatism first emerged, as a clear and distinctive doctrine, almost as early as the French Revolution itself. When Paine wrote *The Rights of Man* in 1793, he was already on the defensive. His work was a refutation of Edmund Burke's *Reflexions on the Revolution in France*, which had appeared in the preceding year. But Burke's conservative position was too well-taken to be disposed of so easily. More than any other single event, the publication of his *Reflexions* helped to bring about a first turning of the revolutionary tide. Against the ideology of liberalism he set up a conservative anti-ideology that laid the essential groundwork for an effective opposition. Largely by his own efforts he managed to turn conservatism into a self-confident and intellectually respectable position. It has since remained a force to be reckoned with in modern politics.

To avoid misunderstanding, a word of explanation may be useful at this point. Language is a living thing, and words are constantly acquiring new meanings. Such shifts of meaning are apt to be particularly wide and rapid in the case of terms that have long been used and abused for purposes of political controversy. "Conservatism" is an extreme but not untypical instance of this. In American politics there has been of late a good deal of interest in something known as the New Conservatism. The main concern of its proponents is to reduce the role of government in American life, and to rely on individual initiative and the free market as the primary agencies of progress. What they advocate, in other words, is the return to an earlier and purer form of the liberal ideology. In most respects this is the exact opposite of the anti-liberal position of Burke and the early conservatives, with which we are now concerned.

CONSERVATIVE ANTI-IDEOLOGY

The conservative reaction to the French Revolution arose in response to liberalism's innovation. Entranced by the expanding vistas of modern science and technology, liberals were disposed to make way for the future by doing away with the past. Their faith in the power of rational invention was so great that they tended to look down on all earlier accomplishments. As the Industrial Revolution soon demonstrated, this confidence in the future was not without foundation. Conservatives argued, however, that, in their preoccupation with the creation of new values, liberals paid too little attention to attendant social costs. Much as people may welcome an improvement in their lot, conservatism insists that happiness also depends on the maintenance of some measure of stability. The breaking of old habits and the learning of new ones is in itself a painful process. For those whose old way of life is threatened, and who lack the special skills and abilities needed for successful adjustment to the new, the pains of innovation may well outweigh its pleasures. The interests of such people were almost wholly neglected by the ideology of early liberalism. Conservatism was the movement that arose in defense of those interests.

To a very large extent, the conservative response to liberalism was not to develop new ideas but to cling to old and long-familiar ways of thought. Against the new ideology many conservatives were simply content to reassert the values of the old order. The duty of obedience to magistrates, clergymen, and other traditional authorities had been inculcated for centuries by the combined forces of church and state. To be content with one's appointed place in the social hierarchy, to do one's duty in the station of life chosen by God had long been the prime requirements of political and social virtue. To abide by these old habits of thought and action was the natural response of those who rejected the liberal revolution. What was needed, however, was a new and vigorous statement of these older pre-liberal ideals. Such a statement, one which would endure to this day, appeared in the 1790s in England.

THE CAREER OF EDMUND BURKE

Edmund Burke was the man who provided the intellectual basis for the conservative reaction. Experience had long prepared him for the performance of this task. Although Burke was an Irishman by birth, he had

made his career in England. By the time of the French Revolution he had
long been recognized as a leading member of the British Parliament. His
life was in some ways strikingly parallel to that of his arch rival, Paine.
Discontented with his own experiences in caste-bound England, Paine
had become an ardent revolutionary who discovered his true homeland
in America; Burke left his native Ireland to find in England his own land
of opportunity. Having won a valued place within the British ruling
classes, he embraced their way of life with all the fervor of a newcomer.
The British Constitution seemed to him the best of constitutions, the
British parliamentary system the best of governments. The values of the
established order were to him a matter of positive faith, not something
just taken for granted. This made him peculiarly sensitive and hostile to
any threat to the maintenance of those values.

Commitment to the principles of the British Constitution did not
mean, however, that Burke was completely opposed to change, or even
to revolution. As a practicing politician he was well aware of the fact that
institutions are in a constant flux of decay and regeneration, and that
drastic measures are sometimes needed to bring them back to health.
Great Britain itself had been through such a crisis in the fairly recent past.
In 1688 the British had gone so far as to expel their reigning king and
to set up a new dynasty with substantially diminished powers. This event
was celebrated, especially by the Whig party, as the Glorious Revolution,
a crucial moment in the defense of British liberties against the encroach-
ments of royal tyranny. Burke himself was a Whig and shared the Whig
tradition. As such he had been, at the time of the American Revolution,
a leading member of that group of British sympathizers who urged that
American grievances be met not by coercion but by conciliation and
compromise.

All this did not prevent him, however, from being one of the very
few people whose reaction to the French Revolution was completely
negative almost from the start. Most foreign observers had been disposed
at first to look on the movement with unabashed enthusiasm. France had
long been notorious, after all, as a politically backward country where
reform was overdue. The English, who for generations had enjoyed many
of the fruits of reform, found it especially easy to assume a benevolent,
elder-brotherly attitude toward the French. Remembering their own revolutionary tradition, the more radical Whigs even went so far as to adopt
the new ideology, and to advocate a correspondingly revolutionary approach to the problems of British politics. This trend of British opinion
in general, and of Whig opinion in particular, quickly aroused Burke's
alarm. At a time when the gravest excesses of the revolutionary movement still lay well in the future, he recognized its radical character and
predicted that its outcome was bound to be a repressive military dictator-

ship. He believed that his fellow countrymen, deluded by the attractions of a revolutionary ideology, were being tempted to destroy the very foundations of the British constitutional tradition. His *Reflexions on the Revolution in France* was a powerful attempt to warn them of that danger.

BURKE'S CHALLENGE TO LIBERAL IDEOLOGY

Although some of Burke's objections to the revolutionary movement were comparatively superficial, the great strength of his book is the fundamental way in which it comes to grips with the problem. With uncommon insight he recognized from the beginning that the really distinctive and dangerous feature of this particular Revolution was the power of its ideology. The core of the revolutionary faith was its supreme confidence in the rational capacities of the individual. It encouraged people to believe that rational self-interest was a sufficient basis for social life, and that the progressive realization of human welfare and happiness was bound to follow as individual thought and action were freed from traditional restraints. Burke's *Reflexions* was a direct and uncompromising attack on that whole position. It tried to show that the rational powers of all individuals, including the most intelligent, are strictly limited; that societies are held together not by the force of reason but by traditional morality and force of habit; and that the progress of civilization, far from being inevitable, is a precarious accomplishment which in turn depends on the maintenance of social order. What Burke did, in other words, was to contradict each and every essential point of the revolutionary theory of progress. Against the ideology of liberalism he erected a conservative anti-ideology. His conservatism was designed as an answer not only to the French Revolution but to ideology in general.

The foundation of Burke's whole argument was his conception of human nature. Great as the power of reason may be, Burke insisted it was not unlimited. As finite beings in an infinite universe, human beings could never hope to know all that they needed to know. The tendency of liberals was to think that they already had, or were about to discover, the answer to every human problem. Burke felt that this was a disastrous overestimate of human rational capacities. Reason, in his opinion, was only half the story. Men and women are not only rational beings; they are also passionate. Irrational drives and impulses are constantly at war with rational judgment. Left to their own devices, human beings would soon come to grief by the unruliness of their passions, destroying both themselves and others in the pursuit of evil purposes. Rational self-interest is very far, therefore, from providing an adequate guide to action. A good deal more is needed for the realization of human purposes.

An Evolutionary View of Social Progress

If humanity is so limited, how can it progress? Burke's answer, typical of conservatism, is that civilization is the outcome of a continuous social process. Even though no one has the capacity to comprehend or resolve any of the larger problems of human existence, most people are intelligent enough to make small but useful experiments within the limits of their own practical experience. Since human beings are social animals, their inconsiderable achievements gain significance in the course of time. They learn from the experiments of their neighbors as well as from their own, and they teach their children useful things that they have come to know. Continued from generation to generation this process leads to a progressive improvement in the human condition. No longer bound by their own personal limitations, human beings profit by an ever-increasing body of useful skills and habits. Social tradition is the force, therefore, that permits humanity to rise above the limitation of its own individual nature. It is the only possible basis for the progress of civilization.

From similar premises, a liberal would have been disposed to conclude that progress is inevitable. Burke, on the contrary, used these arguments to show that civilization itself is a fragile thing, beset by constant dangers. A human being's better self is a product of social discipline, not of individual reason. Left to their own devices, humans would be less than the beasts of the field, who at least have sound instincts to guide them. Strong institutions are needed to repress the selfish and irrational impulses of individuals, and to inculcate civilized habits. But the life of institutions is precarious. A single generation, by rejecting its traditional heritage and failing to pass it on to its descendants, can break the indispensable chain of social continuity, undoing the work of centuries. If humanity is content to maintain and improve its established institutions, progress is perfectly possible. If not, a relapse into barbarism is not only possible, but certain.

The Importance of Traditional Authority

Against this appalling danger, Burke held that there is only one defense: a strong, authoritative government backed by a state-supported church. The state, to be sure, is but one of the many institutions needed for the maintenance of a sound social tradition. A wide variety of private associations, above all the family, is vital to the maintenance of social continuity. Above all, however, the authority of the government stands as the final and indispensable regulator of the whole social process. Only the state has the coercive power needed to regulate the activities of lesser associations, and to repress anti-social conduct. It alone has the resources to support a truly imposing and effective established church, without which

31

there could be, in turn, no secure moral order or social discipline. Far from being, as the liberals would have it, a limited association for limited purposes, the state is an unlimited partnership in which the members of many successive generations unite for the conservation and advancement of their common life as civilized people.

In developing these general principles, Burke's immediate purpose was to refute the particular ideology of the French Revolution. Others saw the Revolution as a liberation of individual energies from needless social restrictions; to him it was a tragic setback in the perennial battle between social welfare and individual selfishness. The fault lay, according to Burke, with the philosophers of the Enlightenment. Presumptuously confident of their own capacity to provide an immediate and perfectly rational solution to all human problems, they had misled a whole generation of French people to destroy their traditional heritage and embark on uncharted courses. Rejecting the possibility of reforming abuses by cautious, piecemeal adjustments, revolutionaries had dared to lay unskilled and inexperienced hands on the fragile fabric of society. All the time-tested structures of church and state had been razed to the ground to make way for new structures. By preferring their own weak reason to the reason of the ages, they had committed the sin of pride and courted fall as the consequence. Once released from their traditional bonds of allegiance, men and women would soon lose the habit of obedience to any rightful authority. Individual passions would know no bounds, submit to none of the hard-won rules of civilized behavior. Such was the frightful price already being paid by the French for accepting a false ideology. Such, too, would be the fate of other peoples who followed their example.

ACHIEVEMENTS AND LIMITATIONS
OF THE CONSERVATIVE REACTION

Burke's *Reflexions* was a work of great eloquence, written in a state of high emotion. As such it suffers the obvious defects of its qualities. Burke himself had little first-hand knowledge of French conditions. His own practical experience was with the British political system, which had already shown in the past, and was thereafter to go on showing, a remarkable capacity for achieving progress within the framework of an essentially conservative tradition. This naturally led him to overestimate the possibilities of conservative reformation in France, where the established order was far more resistant to change, and thus to underestimate the need for revolution. He also tended to exaggerate the costs of revolution. Accurate as he was in predicting military dictatorship and other coming misfortunes, the fate of France never even began to be as dark as he had pictured it. Social customs are tougher, and their roots run deeper, than Burke had dared to imagine. Although the Revolution was a shocking and, in some ways, a crippling experience, it fell far short of destroying the continuity or exhausting the vitality of French civilization. Burke's eloquent picture of the nature and consequences of an ideological movement is not to be taken by any means as the last word on the subject.

When all is said and done, however, the *Reflexions on the Revolution in France* was a remarkable achievement. After nearly 200 years it still stands as the classic model of an eloquent and effective anti-ideology. The ideology of liberalism, when Burke first came to grips with it, was something new and enormously attractive. At a time when many of his fellow Whigs were falling under its spell, Burke rejected liberalism lock, stock and barrel. Without completely rejecting the idea of progress, he argued that evolutionary rather than revolutionary change is the normal means of social development, and that civilization itself depends on the maintenance of at least a certain indispensable minimum of social continuity. His work did much to warn the English of his own day against what he took to be the dangers of revolutionary liberalism, and to confirm their faith in the validity of their own constitutional traditions. It helped to encourage the stubborn British resistance that ultimately led to the downfall of Napoleon and the conservative restoration in Europe. From that day to this, though challenged by much newer ideologies, Burke's philosophy has never lost its position as one of the clearest and most persuasive expressions of the conservative point of view.

CHAPTER FIVE

NATIONALISM

S. Beer

With the collapse of the Napoleonic Empire in 1815, it seemed that
Burke's principles had finally triumphed over the liberalism of Paine.
Conservative monarchies were restored, and the older ruling classes once
again came back into their own. By this time, however, the fight had long
since ceased to be a clear-cut struggle between liberals and conservatives.
Nationalism now was also a factor to be reckoned with. The vigorous
resistance movement which culminated in the overthrow of Napoleon
had been at least as much nationalist as conservative in inspiration, and
had nationalist claims to assert against the monarchs it had rescued. A
generation of imperial glory had also given the French a heightened
sense of national self-consciousness. When Louis XVIII resumed the
throne of his Bourbon ancestors, his first publicly reported statement on
crossing the border was "One more Frenchman is returning to France."
This well-timed piece of publicity was an implicit recognition of the fact
that hereditary right was no longer enough, and that monarchs hence-
forth would do well to appear as representatives of the nation. National
sentiments had already become a formidable force with which all other
doctrines, then and thereafter, would have to make their peace.

That nationalism is a force in the modern world is obvious; to say
what constitutes a nation is much more difficult. Tribal, local, and professional loyalties are easy enough to explain. People who share a common
background have always tended to think of themselves as a group, and
to look on the rest as outsiders. A nation, too, is a self-conscious group,
but one with a character all its own. Typically it is rather large, a good
many million strong, embracing the whole gamut of classes and profes-
sions, and often including a wide variety of regional sub-cultures. Its

members may be divided in their religious affiliations, and may even speak different languages. In spite of all this, however, there is something in their past or present experience that makes them feel as one, all others being lumped together as foreigners. Since the causes of nationality are often hard to see, it can only be defined by its consequences. A nation is a group that, for whatever reason, is so conscious of its distinctiveness that it resents being governed by foreigners and demands a sovereign state of its own. Such demands have played a major role in the development of modern politics.

NATIONALISM
AND THE AGE OF REVOLUTION

Obscure as its origins may be, the growth of nationalism is clearly associated with the rise of ideology. Although the rudiments of national feeling go back much farther, it was long held in check by a powerful sense of respect for traditional authority. Territories were exchanged, by conquest or by inheritance, without regard for the preferences of their inhabitants. All this was changed when liberals began appealing to the authority of the people. They themselves were too rationalistic and too individualistic to be much concerned with national sentiments. Paine was an extreme but not untypical case of liberal cosmopolitanism. Primarily interested in rational principles of government, he was happy to live and work in any country where rational governments were forthcoming. Democracy depends on consensus, however, and most people find it easiest to reach a common agreement with others who feel and act as they do. One of the easiest ways of uniting a people is to set them against another. Paine fostered the growth of American nationalism by preaching hostility to Britain; the Jacobins appealed to French patriotism in their wars against foreign tyrants. Cosmopolitan as they were in their own outlook, they were already discovering the advantages of militant nationalism as a basis for democratic leadership.

For all their nationalistic overtones, however, the French and American revolutions were still largely cosmopolitan and universal movements, offering liberty not to one nation only but to all humanity. As a force clearly opposed to cosmopolitanism, nationalism first came into its own in the ensuing period of resistance to Napoleon. The ever increasing hostility aroused by French imperialism soon made it possible for the surviving traditional monarchies to acquire new popularity. Inspired by national sentiments, patriots from all parts of Germany began rallying in support of Prussia and Austria, the most powerful and independent of the then existing German states, and worked to increase their strength. Spaniards remained faithful to their exiled king and fought his Napoleonic successor with a desperate guerrilla resistance. Even in France, the monarchists were able to make some headway by pointing out that the emperor was a Corsican foreigner with an Italian name, Buonaparte, whereas the Bourbons were truly French. Although nationalism was not the only motive, it undoubtedly played an important part in the coalition of forces that finally unseated Napoleon. Here for the first time, and for time to come, its power was clearly shown.

THE TREND TOWARD
LIBERAL NATIONALISM

Much less clear, however, were the ultimate implications of that power. In the fight against Napoleon, nationalism had associated itself with the cause of conservatism. This association was destined, in part at least, to prove a lasting one. In its emphasis on the values of a specific national heritage, and in its willingness to subordinate individual interests in defense of those values, nationalism betrays a close relationship to the principles of Burkean conservatism. It is therefore not surprising to find that conservatives have generally tended to adopt nationalism as their own, often using the word "national," or some variant thereof, as the official designation of conservative parties. But even so, the partnership has never been complete. The trouble is that nationalism is essentially democratic, an appeal to the will of the people, and the will of the people is not necessarily conservative. A nationalist is typically willing to sacrifice much, including traditional values, to the power and unity of the nation. In the Napoleonic era, for example, the nationalists who rallied to Prussia were also notable reformers. When they felt that traditional usages placed Prussian armies at a disadvantage in competition with the French, they felt no hesitation about abolishing those usages. There can be no guarantee, moreover, that national feeling will coincide with, and thus reinforce, traditional units of government. The nationalism that arose in Germany was not preponderantly Prussian or Austrian nationalism, but German nationalism, which could only be satisfied by the unification of many hitherto independent states. From the very beginning, therefore, nationalism had dynamic implications incompatible with the maintenance of many traditional institutions. This soon led, and still continues to lead, to many a bitter conflict between nationalist and conservative forces.

   The ultimate beneficiary was liberalism. During the period from 1815 to 1848, when conservative governments who joined in a so-called Holy Alliance were making a concerted effort to repress them both, it was natural for liberals and nationalists to make common cause. In this case, too, the alliance was based on shared beliefs as well as on tactical necessities. The common ground here was self-government. For liberals accustomed to thinking of oppressive government as the main enemy of freedom and progress, the struggle of newly emerging nations to throw off their foreign oppressors was bound to seem just. If people have a right to governments of their own choosing, it follows that they have a right to national governments. This argument seemed particularly cogent to Americans, whose own cherished revolution had been a war of national liberation. The right of national self-determination was therefore easy to add to the standard list of accepted liberal principles.

Plausible as it seemed on the surface, however, the acceptance of nationalism was actually a serious breach in the ideological consistency of liberalism. From a liberal standpoint, the principle of national self-determination was allowable only on the assumption that all liberated nations would respect individual liberties and reduce the functions of government to a minimum. This assumption was precarious in fact, and doubtful even in theory. The essence of nationalism, after all, is belief that the interests of the nation, are more important than the interests of any individual, and that government is an indispensable agency for the expression of those interests. In a country like the United States, where devotion to liberal principles has always been an essential part of the national tradition, it makes some sense to speak of liberal nationalism. Elsewhere the phrase comes close to being a paradox, a contradiction of terms.

THE NATIONALISM OF MAZZINI

Perhaps the best way to appreciate the nature of the problem is to examine the writings of an outstanding early nationalist, Giuseppe Mazzini. Mazzini was an Italian patriot, a leading figure in the long and painful struggle to unite the Italian people under a single national government. He was also a general theorist, who believed in national self-determination as a universal principle for the solution of all political problems. In many respects his doctrine sounds like a nationalist version of the liberal ideology. Yet he himself was far from being a liberal. To him, any form of individual self-seeking was rank betrayal of the nation. The title of his most notable essay, *The Duties of Man*, was a deliberate challenge to the liberal principle of individual rights. In an unusually clear and uncompromising way, his work reveals all the difficulties inherent in the liberal-nationalist position.

Its Liberal Aspects

The most liberal aspect of Mazzini's thought is his cosmopolitanism. The liberals had always believed that they were working not for one people only, but for the whole human race. Their ultimate aim was a world of self-governing states peacefully cooperating within the framework of a universal free market, for the welfare and progress of humanity. Mazzini's conception of world order, though couched in more mystical terms, was much the same. Divine providence, he believed, had created a world of separate nations, each, like the children of Israel, with a promised land of its own. This did not mean, however, that the nations were to live in enmity. All men alike are children of God, and therefore brothers. The first duty of every man is to serve God and humanity. Each nation has been endowed divinely with particular characteristics and talents. By cultivating its own gifts within its own territory, each can be expected to make its own distinctive contributions to the common welfare. A world of peacefully cooperating nation states, vying with one another only in desire to be of service to the whole, is the divinely appointed plan for the universal progress of humanity.

In his vision of universal welfare, Mazzini is clearly much indebted to liberalism; his program for realizing that vision brings him even closer to the earlier ideology. For him, as for the liberals, tyrannical governments are the only real enemies of people's progressive destiny. The great majority of individuals, if they could but follow their own natural inclinations, would have no other interest than to serve God and humanity under national governments of their own choosing. At the present time, this cannot be. Tyrannical governments hold people in bondage to monstrous states that disregard the natural limits of nations. Conflicting territorial ambitions lead them to constant wars of aggression. The only cure is for the people to rise up and remake the map of Europe according to the divinely appointed plan. Once the principle of national self-determination has been universally realized, people will no longer be called on to fight one another. The nations therefore will dwell in peace, and their efforts all will be devoted to the common welfare of humanity.

Its Anti-Liberal Aspects

Although Mazzini, in his treatment of international affairs, used the terms "liberty" and "progress" in ways that make him sound like a liberal, the resemblance was superficial. The essential difference was that he was interested in the freedom of national collectivities, not of individuals. The liberals, too, had looked forward to a peaceful and progressive world order, but they had thought of individuals, not social groups, as the primary source of progress. Their world was to have been a place where freedom of thought was universally respected, where intellectual progress was guaranteed by the free exchange of ideas. Economic progress, likewise, was to have come about through the free exchange of goods and services produced by individual enterprise. This faith in progress through individual freedom was alien to Mazzini. According to him, progress was a matter not of individual but of collective action.

Contributions to the welfare of humanity were national contributions, and the only way individuals could serve humanity was by serving their nation. From these premises Mazzini drew conclusions that were basically at variance with the liberal point of view.

The most important case in point is his rejection of freedom of thought. Partly as a result of his fear of Italian regionalism, Mazzini laid great emphasis on national unity. In order to contribute to the progress of humanity, each nation must cultivate its own particular gifts. One of the primary responsibilities of government must be, therefore, to preserve and develop the national character by seeing to it that all citizens share a common national tradition. This calls for an educational system centrally controlled and for the careful suppression of all deviant modes of thought. It is true that progress will depend on the occasional appearance of individuals with new ideas of their own. Such individuals should not be discouraged completely. National unity is the primary consideration, however, and new ideas should not be tolerated if there is any chance that they will endanger the national consensus. The purpose of education is not to create free-thinking individuals but to produce a democratic community symbolized by the love of nation. The duty to the community must always take precedence over the rights of particularistic individuals. The claims of individual self-development, and even of social progress, must always be subordinate to that aim.

In holding to these ideals, Mazzini was heavily influenced by the writings of Rousseau, who believed that nationalism and the democratic commitment to community were preferable to the liberal preoccupation with individuals and their self-interest. In his book *Considerations on the Government of Poland*, Rousseau had advised the Poles to establish national costumes, festivals, and schools in order to instill in its citizens a democratic love of community as opposed to a liberal love of self. He, too, recommended separation from foreigners and close censorship of culture and thought to produce a people committed to the common good. The nation and nationalism, then, became a crucial strategic ally of democratic anti-liberal thought and movements.

Because of his preoccupation with national unity, Mazzini was equally unsympathetic to the idea of economic individualism. A competitive economy encourages individual selfishness and sets brother against brother. It also leads to inequalities of wealth that divide the nation into hostile social classes. All this is quite intolerable. So far as economic life was concerned, Mazzini did not feel, as he did in the case of education, that government control was the answer. Instead he advocated the formation of cooperative associations which, by giving the workers ownership of their own factories and other instruments of production, would eliminate the differences between rich and poor and foster national unity.

This, he felt, would be a vast improvement over the liberal system of individual competition. The importance of this aspect of Mazzini's thought is shown by the fact that *The Duties of Man,* while developing a comprehensive theory of nationalism, was specifically addressed to the needs and interests of the Italian laboring classes. It was conceived not only as a nationalist tract but also as a plea for socialism.

Mazzini was not a typical nationalist in the sense that Paine and Burke may be taken as representative of the liberal and conservative positions. Few of his contemporaries or successors held quite so utopian a view of the benefits to be derived from national self-determination, and many would have rejected, in whole or in part, his anti-liberal conclusions. It is significant that, even in Mazzini's own Italy, it was the liberal monarchy of Piedmont, under the leadership of Cavour, rather than anti-liberal Mazzinians, that finally managed to reach the goal of national reunification. Liberalism and nationalism have proved to be far less antithetical in reality than they are in *The Duties of Man.* But even though the conflict between the two doctrines was not, as Mazzini thought, completely irreconcilable, it was still a genuine conflict. By adopting the principle of national self-determination, the liberal movement exposed itself, along with its victories, to many latent dangers. The nationalism of Mazzini, precisely because it was unusually uncompromising and extreme, had the value of bringing those latent dangers to light.

**THE DIFFICULTIES
OF LIBERAL NATIONALISM**

The first difficulty has to do with the extreme utopianism of the premises on which the idea of national self-determination rests. A glance at *The Duties of Man* should suffice to disabuse anyone who thinks of this as a simple operation. It is true that Mazzini, too, believes it to be simple, but he also spells out, with devastating clarity, the assumptions underlying that belief. God himself has prepared the way by dividing all the peoples of the earth, or at least of Europe, into definite nations, and has assigned to each a national home with definite territorial limits. If this were so, all might indeed be well. In point of fact, however, there are many people whose national allegiances, if any, are uncertain, and it is the exception rather than the rule to find a geographical border that clearly sets apart one nation from another. Under these circumstances, any attempt to apply the principle of national self-determination is bound to lead to endless difficulties. Commitment to that principle has not simplified, but greatly complicated, the problems of international life.

Mazzini's hope for a future world order rests on the assumption that no nation will be tempted to make special claims for itself at the expense of any other. This is a good deal to ask of people who are supposed to be completely absorbed in and devoted to a particular national tradition. It is significant that Mazzini himself, when he imagined a future congress of nations, immediately assumed that the congress would meet in Rome, and recognize Italy as its leader. For all his belief in humanity and the brotherhood of all people, his patriotism was too great to allow him to think of Italy as being no better than other nations.

It was not, however, in the international field that nationalism was to prove most damaging to the future of liberalism; the original purity of its ideology was much more seriously compromised by the results that followed in the field of domestic politics. The essence of liberalism had always been its faith in individual action. Its formula for progress was to reduce the functions of government to a minimum, thus leaving people free to follow the dictates of rational self-interest. By accepting the principle of nationalism, the liberals introduced a radically alien element into what up to then had been a simple, self-consistent system. In the case of the nation, they had for the first time recognized the existence of a social entity with claims to a life of its own. For any true nationalist, however liberal, the interests of the nation were bound to take precedence over the interests of mere individuals. The individual was displaced from the center of the stage, which marks the beginning of the end of liberalism as a pure and self-consistent ideology.

CHAPTER SIX

SOCIALISM

natl socialism = fascism

cf 36

When Mazzini tried, in 1840, to preach the gospel of nationalism to Italian workers, he was careful to show that his doctrine was not liberal but socialistic. This was not just a matter of personal preference; he also took it for granted that this was the right way to make an appeal for working-class support. Far from being a novelty, his assumption was already commonplace, for by then liberalism had long since lost its monopoly as the only widely acceptable form of modern ideology. Liberalism had had its heyday in the eighteenth century; in the nineteenth century, socialism had emerged as the new wave of the future. To be sure, the nineteenth century brought forth no socialist counterpart to the French Revolution, and when a comparable revolution, in 1917, did at last occur in Russia, one could argue that the socialism that emerged was altered by historical necessity. But even though it never reached its ultimate objectives, the socialist movement was a force to be reckoned with. As time went on, the adherents of liberalism, conservatism, and other rival doctrines found increasingly, as Mazzini had done, that socialism was one of the basic components of modern political thought.

THE ORIGINS OF SOCIALISM:
LOSS OF FAITH IN THE FREE MARKET

Socialism arose from the failure of liberalism. It came from the inability of liberalism to live up to its own most optimistic promises of economic welfare. According to the theorists of the free market, the elimination of governmental restrictions on trade and manufacture would lead to an immediate and universal improvement in the material conditions of life.

Real wealth did increase at an unprecedented rate, and the equally unprecedented increase of population showed that at least some of the
benefits of the Industrial Revolution were being widely shared. What
most impressed contemporary observers, however, was the economic
inequalities engendered in the process. Only the relatively rich and enterprising were in a position to take full advantage of the new economic
order. Successful bankers and market speculators grew spectacularly rich,
while the lot of the slum-dwelling working classes showed little if any
improvement. This was a bitter disappointment to the humanitarian
hopes of those who had embraced liberalism in the expectation that the
benefits of economic progress would be shared by all humanity. Socialism
arose as a response to this disappointment.

   Since economic inequality seemed to be the inevitable consequence
of free competition, the proponents of equality naturally began to look
on the free market itself as the primary obstacle to human welfare. Like
the liberals before them, the socialists were believers in progress. They
too were confident that there was practically no limit to what people could
accomplish if they were allowed to give free expression to their natural
creative capacities. They differed from their predecessors in their esti-
mate of the reason why men and women were unable, under present
circumstances, to realize their true potential. For the liberals, legal and
political inequalities alone had seemed to be the main barrier to self-
realization; for the socialists, economic inequalities were the main difficulty. To eliminate market competition, the source of those inequalities,
was the essential objective of the socialist movement.

   The first stirrings of socialism date back to the days of the French
Revolution itself. Although the great majority of the revolutionists had
been content to abolish legal inequalities among citizens, there were
already a few who were convinced that this was not enough. The revolutionary slogan "Liberty, Equality, Fraternity" would be meaningless, they
felt, as long as French citizens were divided from one another by inequalities of wealth. Under the leadership of Babeuf, some of them went so far
as to conspire to seize the government and carry the work of the revolution to its logical economic conclusions. Although the effort was feeble
and easily suppressed, it came to be regarded by later generations of
socialists as prophetic of things to come.

UTOPIAN SOCIALISM

It was not, however, until the first decades of the nineteenth century that
socialism began in earnest. Those decades saw a remarkable efflores-
cence of socialist thought, especially in France and Britain. Although
these early writers are often lumped together as the "Utopians," they

actually represented the widest possible variety of opinions. Some, like Saint-Simon and Louis Blanc, advocated a more or less centralized economy under state control. Others hoped to solve the "social question" by various forms of private association. One popular notion, to which the word "utopian" most properly applies, was to escape from the rigors of the industrial age by withdrawing to self-sufficient communities in which men, women, and children would satisfy all their needs, without resorting to the market, on a basis of free cooperation.

The two outstanding proponents of this position were Owen and Fourier. Robert Owen (1771–1858), a Scottish cotton manufacturer, believed that in a reconstructed community people could be taught the principles of cooperation instead of competition. Human nature could be remade if the environment were restructured. His ideas were widely popular for a time. Model communities committed to harmony and cooperation sprang up in Scotland, England, and throughout America. Charles Fourier (1772–1837), a Frenchman, had an immensely more detailed plan for a model community—a phalanstery, as he called it. In it, Fourier saw all humanity realizing its potential. Waste, inefficiency, boredom, and inequality would be eliminated in the planned, non-competitive environment of the phalanstery. A world aware of such utopian existence would be persuaded to mend its ways and would, Fourier assured, be converted to communitarian socialism.

An idea of more lasting importance was that of Pierre Joseph Proudhon (1809–1865), who hoped to set up a nationwide system of decentralized workers' cooperatives, which would bargain with one another for the mutual exhange of goods and services. It is hard to think of writers so widely different as part of a single movement. All were agreed, however, on one main point: they all believed that individual enterprise and market competition were inimical to human welfare and would have to be replaced by a more cooperative form of social organization. Even though none of these doctrines won much of a permanent following, their persistence was symptomatic of a growing discontent.

In 1848, when conservative monarchies everywhere were forced into retreat, the socialists were already strong enough to play an appreciable, if minor, part in the ensuing revolutionary disturbances, especially in France. Proudhon was elected to the National Assembly, and Louis Blanc was even authorized temporarily to set up national workshops for the relief of unemployment. All this came to nothing much, however. The trouble was that there was a plethora of socialist ideas, but nothing yet that amounted to a full-fledged ideology. At the time of the French Revolution, the liberals knew exactly what they wanted. They all were agreed, and had inspired a wide popular following to believe, that the elimination of unequal legal and political privileges would inevitably clear the way to unprecedented progress. Although the socialists of 1848 also thought they knew what was wrong with the world, they were still far from having reached any common conclusion as to what to do about it. Without a simple and clear-cut promise of their own to offer, they could hardly hope to persuade the masses to join them in a new revolutionary movement.

THE SCIENTIFIC SOCIALISM
OF MARX AND ENGELS

Karl Marx was the man who finally succeeded in providing socialism with an effective ideology. Both he and his close collaborator, Friedrich Engels, were Germans who spent most of their active lives in England, the homeland of the Industrial Revolution. Like most of the early socialists, they were middle-class intellectuals. Humanitarian sympathy, not personal experience, was what led them to devote their lives to the cause of the working classes. Before going to England, Marx had spent some time in Paris and had become acquainted with many of the leaders of French socialism. Although he sympathized with their objectives, he considered their methods absurdly amateurish. Their theories were arbitrary constructions that had no sound and demonstrable connection with the facts of social life. Marx himself was a well-trained academic philosopher, much concerned with questions of method. What socialism needed, in his opinion, was a truly scientific theory, a theory which would prove that the destruction of the existing social order was not only desirable, but also inevitable. To create a theory of this sort became his life ambition.

In carrying out his program, however, he had to overcome one main obstacle. Partly as a result of the conservative reaction, the intellectual climate of Marx's time was far less favorable to theories of revolution than it had been in the preceding century. People now were disposed to emphasize the continuity of social life, and to think of social change as a matter of gradual evolution. Though radical in their ultimate objectives, most socialists had assumed that it would be necessary to approach their goal by slow and piecemeal efforts. More firmly even than the others, Marx too believed that history is a determinate and continuous process. One of the outstanding achievements of the Hegelian school of philosophy, in which he himself had been reared, had been to create a philosophy of history. He also believed, however, that nothing less than a thoroughgoing revolutionary upheaval would suffice to destroy the existing order. The continuity of history had not prevented the liberals, after all, from rising to power by way of the French Revolution. Marx's problem was to show that the course of historical evolution would soon, and inevitably, give the working classes a similar occasion for successful revolutionary action.

DIALECTICAL MATERIALISM

The principle of "dialectical materialism" was his answer to the problem. "Dialectical" was a term borrowed from the technical vocabulary of philosophy, and Marx's use of it shows how much his theory owed to his training as a philosopher. The word originally referred to the process whereby ideas are formed and clarified in the course of intellectual debate. A proposition, or thesis, is first advanced, and then challenged by a counter-proposition, or antithesis. Since both are apt to be partly true, the normal outcome of the ensuing discussion is a revised proposition, or synthesis, that combines the valid elements of each. Dialectical materialism is an attempt to show that the historical development of social institutions follows the same pattern. The principle of materialism, as Marx interprets it, is that the driving force in human life is economic, the quest for material welfare. The essential purpose of all ideas and institutions—political, religious, or economic—is to safeguard economic interests. At any given stage of economic development there is a ruling class which, by monopolizing the ownership of land, factories, or other sources of wealth, is in a position to dominate the whole of society. Great as its power may be, however, it is basically unstable. In the course of time, new sources of wealth are discovered and lead to new forms of economic organization. New classes arise to exploit these opportunities, thus challenging the monopoly of the older ruling class. Dialectically speaking, the established order is a thesis that inevitably produces its own antithesis in the form of a new, revolutionary class. The result is a revolutionary crisis, or synthesis, in which the new class, having gradually grown stronger than the old, overthrows its former rulers and completely refashions society in accordance with its own interests. History, in other words, is a dialectical process, in which each period of evolutionary growth is bound to culminate in revolution. Dialectical materialism is the term Marx used to characterize this inexorable course of development.

Confidence in the dialectic made it possible for Marx to predict things to come, with an assurance unknown to most of his fellow socialists. The ruling class of the moment were the capitalists—the merchants and manufacturers who owned the factories, banks, and other institutions that dominated the economic life of the age inaugurated by the Industrial Revolution. In the French Revolution they had broken the regime of their former rules, the aristocrats, whose power, based on the once all-important ownership of land, was no longer a match for their own. All the political and social institutions of the time, including the schools, the churches, the press, and other agencies in control of public opinion, had been shaped to serve their interest. Strong as they were, however, their days were already numbered. The new industrial order, as a thesis, had inevitably produced its own antithesis, the factory workers or, as the socialists preferred to call them, the proletariat. Men and women who had nothing but their own labor to sell had no choice but to work for wages, on terms set by the capitalists, whose ownership of all the significant instruments of production gave them a monopoly of the labor market. The latter held wages down to a starvation level, and appropriated to themselves in the form of surplus value, or profits, the greater part of the wealth that their workers were producing. As an exploited class, the proletarians were bound to grow ever more conscious of their common interest in opposing the capitalists. The nature of capitalism was such, moreover, that the power of the proletariat, according to Marx, was steadily increasing. In a competitive economy, successive waves of weaker capitalists were being forced out of business by richer and more efficient competitors, and driven down into the ranks of the proletariat. The inevitable outcome would be that an ever larger and stronger proletariat would finally succeed, by sheer weight of numbers, in overwhelming an ever smaller and weaker capitalist class. When this happened there would be a new revolutionary crisis, and the factory workers, like the French Revolutionists before them, would have the opportunity to create a dialectical synthesis of their own.

THE POST-REVOLUTIONARY UTOPIA

Marx did more, however, than to promise victory; he also gave the proletarians reason to believe that theirs was destined to be not just one revolution among many, but a final and decisive achievement. In so doing he reached a degree of utopianism which outdoes even the most optimistic hopes of his liberal predecessors. Although the latter believed in minimizing the use of coercion, they had generally agreed that there are limits to the spontaneous sociability of people, and that the coercive authority of governments would always be needed to settle disputes and to safeguard life and property. Marx made no such concessions to any permanent human frailty. To his way of thinking, the final outcome of the destruction of capitalism would be the establishment, once and for all, of a perfect classless society. This society would be so peaceful and cooperative that there would no longer be any need for coercion. All questions would be settled by rational agreement. No longer needed, the state with all its coercive powers would disappear forever.

Marx's proof of these propositions followed quite simply from his premises. According to the principle of materialism, the only significant causes of social conflict are clashes of economic interest. As long as society is divided into separate classes, the ruling class will always need a coercive state to defend its special privileges. When the proletarians come to power, they too will set up a state of their own, a dictatorship of the proletariat, to protect their class interests. Unlike the governments of the past, however, that served oppressive minorities, the proletarian distatorship will be a government by and for the great oppressed majority. Its purpose will be to seize the property of the capitalist minority. Private owners of the instruments of production will then cease to exist. Ownership will be vested in society as a whole and used for common purposes. Since class differences depend on differences in the ownership of property, the result of common ownership will be to produce a one-class, or classless, society. The only purpose of government is to permit one class to coerce another. From this it follows that, in a classless society, the state will have no functions to perform, and will slowly wither away.

ALIENATION AND SPECIES BEING

Marx never spelled out in great detail what life would be like in the socialist utopia of classless society. There are several reasons for this failure. Marx felt that utopian socialists devoted too much energy to minute descriptions of the future instead of seeking to get there. Moreover, detailed descriptions of objectives encouraged compromise with clever reactionary politicians. Finally, Marx held that, since humanity had never before experienced such an existence, it was beyond its capacity even to contemplate the new order. All of this notwithstanding, Marx's earliest philosophical writings indicate that he foresaw a fundamental transformation in human nature occurring with the collectivization of property and the elimination of wage slavery.

The actuality of human existence would be replaced by the potentiality of human essence. Leaning heavily on the philosophical formulations of his great mentor, Hegel, Marx was convinced that the reality for workers under capitalism was alienation, estrangement from their real selves, from their real potential as species beings, as true members of the human race. Workers were separated from their work; they were mere automatons, mere indistinguishable things in the process of production. Workers were also estranged from the product of their work. They had no control over what was done with what they had made. They were also cut off from their fellow human beings, as capitalism rendered them competitive with and hostile to each other. Most significant of all, the workers were alienated from their species, their potential as human beings. Men and women were distinct from other animals because they toiled not only to subsist and reproduce, but also to lead creative and interesting lives. Capitalism denied them their species character as wage slavery reduced humanity to the level of other animals.

The true potential of humanity—its species quality—would only be realized, according to Marx, when the means of production were collectivized, when the economic expropriation of the worker's surplus value by the capitalist was ended. Human alienation would forever be ended only when socialized production was matched by socialized appropriation. Marx thus envisioned a complete and utter revolutionary transformation of human personality. It was ideological utopianism in its most brilliant, unalloyed expression.

THE AMBIGUITIES AND ACHIEVEMENTS
OF SCIENTIFIC SOCIALISM

Although Marx believed that his doctrine, unlike that of the utopians, was a strictly "scientific" socialism, it actually depended on some very critical assumptions. A host of crucial ambiguities lay hidden, for example, in his concept of a classless society. His vision of the future was meaningful only on the assumption that the capitalists alone had special interests, and that the interests of the proletariat were identical with those of all the rest of the population. In terms of Marx's own principle of materialism, this was more than doubtful. The class composition of modern society, as he himself recognized, is highly complicated. The large agrarian sector of the economy, in particular, with its landlords, tenants, independent farmers, and hired workers, involves a whole series of productive relationships that have little to do with the problems of factory workers. In spite of all this, Marx believed that a large majority of the rural population would come, sooner or later, to identify themselves with the proletariat.

Even as applied to factory workers, moreover, Marx's concept of a unified proletariat was far from being clear. He generally speaks as if the mere experience of economic exploitation would suffice to give all the factory workers a common class consciousness in opposition to their employers. But he also perceived astutely that the capitalists, with the aid of schools, churches, and newspapers, and backed by the coercive power of the state, have a considerable capacity to deceive the working classes and thus to prevent them from recognizing their true interests. Marx often finds it necessary, therefore, to distinguish between the proletariat, in general, and the "class-conscious" proletariat. And the situation is still further complicated by the fact that not all members of the class-conscious proletariat are necessarily proletarians. Middle-class intellectuals may well be able to rise above their former class prejudices and devote themselves to the proletarian cause because of their particular objectivity and insight. Marx and Engels themselves are outstanding examples. Such people are presumably included in the "vanguard" of the proletariat, another group of proletarians whom Marx occasionally mentions.

The ambiguities of Marx's class concept proved in the long run to be the source of many difficulties. Above all, they made it hard to determine whether and, if so, to what extent, the Marxists were committed to democratic principles. Economically and socially, the implications of the doctrine were clearly democratic, inasmuch as the future dictatorship of the proletariat was envisaged as a government exercised in the name and in the interests of an overwhelming majority of the population. Marx never really specified, however, that it was also to be a government *by* the people, in the full democratic sense of effective majority control. Would the revolution have to wait until the minority of factory workers had won enough adherents from other economic classes to constitute an absolute majority, or would it be proper for them to set up a minority government in the interests of all? Should the vanguard wait until the whole proletariat had become actively class-conscious; or should it proceed, whenever the time seemed ripe, to dictate over backward proletarians? The writings of Marx and Engels give no answer to such questions. Controversies over these very issues were destined, in later years, to do much to impair the unity of the socialist movement.

For all their future importance, however, these latent tensions did little to impair the ideological effectiveness of Marxism. By adhering to this doctrine, the socialists gained a fighting faith which in no way suffered by comparison with the ideology of liberalism. To members of the lower classes, its ideal of a classless society was much more appealing than the liberal ideal of free competition. Its formula for achieving that goal, by a revolutionary confiscation of private capital, was a clear and simple one. Its claims to scientific inevitability won it high standing in an age much given to the awed and uncritical acceptance of scientific achievements. In Marxism, all the essential features of a modern ideology were combined to arouse the hopes of people no longer content with the fading promise of liberalism. Socialism had emerged as a major force in the world of modern politics.

CHAPTER SEVEN

THE EVOLUTION OF LIBERALISM

While in many ways the Age of Ideology reached its high-water mark with the rise of Marxian socialism, liberalism was by no means dead. The nineteenth century saw its realization in England, its original home. By the middle of the nineteenth century England had long been recognized, in most respects, as the leading liberal nation. The most highly industrialized of all countries, it was also the most consistent in its support of free trade and in its defense of personal liberties. Much of the credit for this was due to a small but highly influential group of liberal ideologists. Ever since the days of Adam Smith, the British school of classical economists had been the mainstay of economic liberalism. Other aspects of liberal doctrine were well represented by Jeremy Bentham and his associates, the Utilitarians. Inspired by a typically ideological faith in the power of human reason, the Benthamites advocated a wide variety of radical reforms. The strength of the British constitutional tradition was so great, however, that they had been content to implement their program by parliamentary rather than by revolutionary action. This gave them some understanding of, and respect for, the ordinary give and take of parliamentary negotiation. It was therefore relatively easy for them to modify their ideological commitments and to adopt a more realistic attitude toward politics.

JOHN STUART MILL

The most interesting theorist in this connection is John Stuart Mill. His father, a high-ranking employee of the British East India Company, was a well-known Utilitarian. Since the younger Mill was something of an infant prodigy, great care was lavished on his education in the hope and expectation that he would follow in his father's footsteps. This, to a very large extent, he actually proceeded to do. He too earned his living at India House and yet managed, in his spare time, to produce a body of writings that gave him an early and lasting reputation as the outstanding liberal theorist of the mid-nineteenth century. His *Principles of Political Economy* long held the field as the leading textbook of classical economics, and his essay *On Liberty* still holds an outstanding place among statements of the case for free speech. But even though he remained faithful, in most respects, to his Utilitarian upbringing, he was also open to other influences. His wide acquaintanceship among intellectuals of all sorts, including Mazzini, did much to broaden his sympathies and caused him to qualify some of the more simple-minded assumptions of his predecessors. As compared with the latter, he also enjoyed the useful advantage of hindsight. Many of the changes for which his father and other early liberals had worked were now fact, and could be judged by their consequences. For a man as intelligent as Mill, there was no lack of material by which to test and modify the earlier ideology.

The Problem of Majority Rule

The most distinctive feature of Mill's final position, as compared with that of his predecessors, was a basic reassessment of the problem of democracy. To Bentham and the elder Mill, majority rule seemed the best of all possible governments. Like Paine, they assumed that the masses would generally be reasonable enough to appreciate the advantages of the liberal version of freedom. John Stuart Mill was also a democrat by conviction. For him, the right of self-government was not just a utilitarian convenience, but a moral necessity, indispensable to the attainment of man's proper goal of self-determination. So great, indeed, was his belief in the moral significance of responsible political action, that he became one of the earliest advocates of woman's suffrage. His faith in the moral value of democracy was combined, however, with an acute awareness of the practical dangers implicit in mass action. Far from believing in the inevitable goodness and rationality of majorities, he felt that the normal impulses of ordinary men and women were inimical to freedom. For him, the acceptance of democratic principles was not a panacea but a problem.

Since Mill was an intellectual, he was naturally much concerned about the question of intellectual freedom. His great fear of the masses was that they would use their power to discourage or prohibit uncommon lines of thought and action, forcing everyone to conform to a common standard of popular mediocrity. In this he was much influenced by Alexis de Tocqueville, whose book *Democracy in America* had made a great impression on contemporary thought. In his famous study of the world's first great experiment in mass democracy, the French aristocrat had laid great emphasis on the overriding uniformity of American life, and had remarked on the peculiar unwillingness of Americans to tolerate individuals or groups who tried to live lives or think thoughts of their own. Mill found in this an ominous parallel to what he himself had seen of life in mid-Victorian England. Though the effects of mass democracy were only just beginning to be felt in that country, the pressure for social conformity was already much in evidence. Along with the Industrial Revolution, a new and stringent code of behavior, known as Victorian morality, had laid hold on merry England. Although Mill himself was far from being a man of Bohemian habits, he was alarmed by the growing tendency to standardize people's lives. Diversity and experiment, he firmly believed, are essential to human progress. He felt that the masses, in their lazy and unthinking devotion to familiar ways, were in danger of drying up the vital sources of all truly progressive achievement.

Mill on Liberty

The purpose of the essay *On Liberty* was to draw attention to this problem and to show that individual freedom ought to be protected. In support of this proposition, Mill adopted two parallel lines of argument, the first Utilitarian and the second non-Utilitarian in character. He defended freedom of thought and discussion, in the first place, on the ground that it is useful to society. Rational knowledge is the basis of social welfare, and the only way of confirming and extending true knowledge is to submit all ideas, old or new, to the test of free discussion and debate. So far, Mill's argument has the familiar ring of eighteenth-century liberalism. His second line of defense, on the other hand, is entirely different from the first. Quite apart from the question of social utility, he tries to show that individual self-determination is a basic human right, indispensable to the development of any sort of moral responsibility. No line of thought or action, objectively true and useful though it may be, is morally significant unless it is followed, freely and consciously, as a matter of personal conviction. Without liberty to choose between conflicting claims, a human being loses his or her rightful dignity as a moral and rational being. This second argument is the core of Mill's particular variety of liberalism.

That the author is more concerned with moralistic than with Utilitarian considerations is reflected in the preponderantly individualistic tenor of his writings. The main proposition set forth in his essay *On Liberty* is that society has a right to regulate "other-regarding" actions, but that "self-regarding" actions are none of its business. The rights of the individual, in the latter case, are absolute, and do not depend in any way on the principle of social utility. This is, in itself, a meaningless proposition, for the distinction between self-regarding and other-regarding actions is not at all self-evident. There are very few things that a person can do purely on his or her own account, without having some effect on other people. For anyone disposed to emphasize the social consequences of individual action, there are no imaginable extremes of social regulation that could not be justified in accordance with Mill's principle. But Mill himself approached the matter from the opposite direction. According to him, the burden of proof lies squarely and heavily on the proponents of social action. The normal assumption must be that men and women have a right to live their own lives. An action is other-regarding, and therefore subject to regulation, only when it has a decisively adverse effect on the freedom of other people. Social consequences of an indirect and unsubstantial character do not suffice to prevent the acts of an individual from being classed as self-regarding. The whole purpose of Mill's argument was to narrow the claims that might properly be made in the name of social utility, and to secure recognition, as far as possible, for the right of individual self-determination.

This was all very well as a statement and justification of liberal objectives, but how were they ever going to be reached? Earlier liberals had had an easy answer to this question. Because of their faith in the essential rationality of men, they had been able to go forward in the serene assurance that liberal truths, once stated, were bound to prevail. Mill could not. His motive in writing *On Liberty* had been to defend the rights of exceptional individuals against the blindness and hostility of ordinary people. In so doing he was well aware of the fact that no words of his could do much to improve the situation. Stupid and prejudiced people are not likely to be moved by the force of rational arguments. There is no assurance, as Mill pointed out, that truth will prevail over falsehood, even in the long run. For a truly liberal society to come into existence, the groundwork must be laid by a careful program of social and political action. To spell out the requirements of such a program was the ultimate objective of Mill's political thought.

The Problem of Education

One likely approach to the matter was by way of education. The best time to shape people's attitudes was in their early and formative years. Mazzini had relied on this principle when he advocated a uniform system of state education for the inculcation of nationalism. Although Mill, with his emphasis on freedom and diversity, was naturally disposed to prefer private over public education, he too believed that the state had a right to insist on minimum educational standards for all its citizens. Unlike Mazzini's, his purpose was not to inculcate common beliefs, but to teach people to think for themselves. The state should guarantee that all children had the opportunity to acquire literacy and other elementary tools of thought. Through exposure to the basic methods and attitudes of objective scientific inquiry, their native intelligence should be so well schooled that they could be trusted thereafter to follow their own bent in a fairly reasonable fashion. Mill was too realistic to think of liberal education as a cure for every evil. He regarded it, however, as a necessary prerequisite for life in a free society.

Unexceptionable as this conclusion might be, it threatened to leave Mill face to face with a hopeless vicious circle. An enlightened electorate called for an enlightened educational policy supported by the government. According to Mill's own principles of self-determination and moral responsibility, governments ought to be democratic. Democratic action is dependent on the will of a mass electorate. Only an enlightened electorate could be expected to support a policy of liberal education. Our initial proposition was, however, that mass electorates will *not* be enlightened unless they have already had a liberal education. Thus the argument comes circling around, back to its starting point, and leaves the state of things no better than it was at the beginning.

The Creation of an Enlightened Electorate

The only way to escape the difficulty, without sacrificing liberal principles, is to abandon strict adherence to democracy, and this is exactly what Mill did. Even though liberalism might be committed to the proposition that all people ought to share in the responsibilities of self-government, it did not necessarily follow that they ought to do so immediately. For the time being, it might be wiser to leave power in the hands of a relatively experienced and well-educated elite. Under the tutelage of a liberal-minded minority, the masses could slowly acquire the various skills needed for effective citizenship. As their education progressed, their political responsibilities would increase in like proportion. The final outcome would be a completely free society in which all men and women had an equal share in the rights and duties of government. Then, and then only, would it be possible to bring liberalism and democracy together in effective partnership.

This was the general argument that Mill set forth in his essay *On Representative Government.* One of the more notable features of this work is its plan for the gradual extension of the franchise. The method itself, and the reasons given to justify it, are precisely the same as those regularly used by British colonial administrations when they first began to introduce their imperial charges to the responsibilities of government. Untutored people, so the argument runs, cannot be trusted to vote wisely in national elections. The needs of the nation as a whole are too complex to be understood at once. Local governments, on the other hand, have fewer powers and deal with simple matters. In educating a mass electorate, therefore, the proper procedure is to start by allowing people to vote on local matters only. Under conditions laid down by the national authorities, and with the aid and advice of national officials, the inhabitants of a particular locality can be entrusted with the management of their own affairs. Through practical experience, their skill and wisdom will gradually increase. Their growth in political capacity will find its reward in progressively larger grants of power. If all goes well, they will finally gain admission to the national electorate as fully qualified citizens. Mill recommended this procedure not for colonial peoples only, but for all those who hope to reach the goal of democratic government.

The Virtues of Representative Government

Even under the best of conditions, however, Mill feared that mass electorates would never be really reliable. His real hope for the future lay in the fact that the only possible form of modern democracy is representative government. Unlike the citizens of the ancient city states, who transacted public business in mass assemblies, modern electorates act indirectly, through representatives of their own choosing. These representatives are usually well above the average in ability and experience, much more amenable than the masses to rational persuasion. According to Mill, the quality of representative assemblies would be still higher if intelligent minorities were enabled to combine their votes under a system of proportional representation. In any case, the chances were that the intellectual elite would carry greater weight among representatives of the people than they would among the people themselves. Mill therefore advocated representative government, with all its limitations, as the best possible means through which to seek the goal of a truly free society.

As compared with the position of the earlier Utilitarians, Mill's writings mark a decisive change in the current of liberal thought. The change was a matter not so much of content as of method. The freedoms Mill cherished were essentially the same as those of his predecessors. Though his economic views, as he set them forth in the *Principles of Political Economy,* made some small concessions to the need for state intervention, his devotion to the free market stood squarely within the tradition of the classical economists. In his emphasis on personal freedoms he was, if anything, even more libertarian than the earlier liberals had been. What set him apart was his conception of the nature and limitations of the political means available for the accomplishment of liberal purposes. Liberalism, for him, has already lost much of its ideological character. Far from offering a quick and total solution to the problems of human existence, it is a distant objective which can only be realized, and thereafter defended, by unremitting effort. The minority who espouse it cannot expect to win ready popular acceptance. To make it a reality they must be content to work for piecemeal accomplishments by a constant process of parliamentary negotiation. Twentieth-century liberalism, with its endless compromises and adjustments to opposing points of view, is already clearly implicit in Mill's revision of the liberal position.

CHAPTER EIGHT

POLITICAL CATHOLICISM

More striking, even, than the evolution of modern liberalism was the change of political attitudes that occurred during the course of the nineteenth century within the Roman Catholic Church. Since World War I, Catholic parties have often collaborated with liberals and socialists in support of constitutional democracy. A hundred years earlier it would have been impossible to imagine any such development. In 1818 the Catholic Church was thoroughly identified with the conservative reaction. The French Revolution was anathema, liberalism the most dangerous of heresies. Good Catholics were expected to work and pray for the absolute monarchs whose powers had been so recently restored.

THE CATHOLIC-CONSERVATIVE ALLIANCE

It is easy enough to see why Catholics should have started off in alliance with the conservatives. For centuries past the church had been an integral part of the established political order. The French Revolution had gravely impaired its former wealth and standing. The early liberals were generally anti-clerical, often anti-Christian. When the socialist movement came along, it worsened the situation. The Marxists, in particular, were enthusiastic atheists, who looked on the church as part of the capitalist world that was slated for extinction. Only the conservatives were disposed to respect the traditional rights of the church. Under these circumstances, it seemed prudent for faithful Catholics to adopt a conservative position.

A good deal more than expediency was involved, however, in the church's hostile reaction to the Age of Ideology. Its basic philosophical

58

and religious convictions, as well as its more superficial interests, were profoundly threatened by the rise of the liberal and socialist movements. Both ideologies proclaimed a truly overwhelming confidence in the powers of human reason. Their promise for the future rested explicitly on the proposition that individuals, by giving full and uninhibited play to their rational powers, are capable of making discoveries that will lead to the establishment of something not very far removed from a kingdom of heaven on earth. This stands as a direct and irreconcilable challenge to the promise of Christianity.

The Catholics, too, have faith in human reason, but that faith is strictly qualified. Although humans are rational creatures, they are also creatures of sin. As a consequence of the fall of Adam, their original nature has been so gravely impaired that they are no longer capable of fulfilling the functions assigned to them as a part of God's all-embracing plan for a perfect universe. It is only by the special grace of God that they can now overcome their deficiencies. By accepting the truths that God himself has revealed to his one true church, and by participating in its sacraments, people can hope to remedy their condition here on earth, and to enjoy a blissful life hereafter. Without the assistance of God and the church, human reason is incapable of reaching its true perfection. For humans to dream of achieving a kingdom of heaven on earth, by their own unaided efforts, is wicked and reckless presumption.

THE IDEA OF A
CHRISTIAN COMMONWEALTH

From the Catholic standpoint, the most reasonable form of society is a Christian commonwealth. Church and state alike are institutions ordained by God for the welfare of humanity. The relationship between them ought to be one of close cooperation. The function of the church is to teach the truth and to administer the sacraments; the function of the state is to maintain order and to enforce justice. On questions related to faith and morals, the state ought to defer to the authority of the church and aid in its rightful work of repressing sin and heresy. The church, in return, should defer to the authority of the state in secular matters and teach the people that to disobey or rebel against legitimate rulers is a sin in the eyes of God. People are so sinful by nature that they need strong guidance to keep them from straying. Only in a Christian commonwealth, where church and state work hand in hand, can they hope to be given a reasonable opportunity of following the road to eventual salvation.

Under the conditions of nineteenth-century politics, conservatism was the natural allegiance for anyone who shared this point of view. Liberals believed, as a matter of principle, in the separation of church and state. Under a liberal regime, the best the church could look forward to was religious freedom and the right to compete on equal terms with teachers of falsehood and error. The socialists were even worse. What they promised was not official neutrality and toleration, but open persecution. Only the conservatives still believed in the idea of a Christian commonwealth. Although monarchs of the post-Napoleonic era had been forced to make some liberal gestures toward freedom of thought and religion, their hearts were generally in the right place. They supported their traditional church establishments, Protestant or Catholic as the case might be, and encouraged them in their efforts to put down all dangerous thoughts and actions. Under the conservatives there could still be some hope of returning to Christian principles of social organization. To aid them was a sacred duty for all right-thinking followers of God and the Catholic Church.

THE FAILURE OF CONSERVATISM

Reasonable as this policy seemed to its followers, it was doomed to disappointment. In identifying itself with absolute monarchy, the church had tied its fortunes to a losing cause. Liberalism, nationalism, and socialism were the rising forces of the time, and all were working to overthrow the conservative reaction. All during the first half of the nineteenth century, revolutionary outbreaks were frequent. In 1830 conservative monarchies were overthrown in a number of countries, most notably France, and replaced by liberal regimes. The more widespread disturbances of 1848, and the national unification of Germany and Italy in 1870, completed the undoing of the conservative post-Napoleonic settlement. From then on, the only way for a monarchy to survive in Western Europe was to accept the principles of liberal constitutionalism. Absolute rulers were no longer available to support a Christian commonwealth.

The result was a dangerous crisis in the life of the church. For generations the Catholics had been identified with conservative and traditional interests. This policy was now clearly bankrupt. Although conservatism still retained considerable strength in many rural communities, it had little appeal for the ever-growing urban populations that had risen to preponderance with the growth of modern industry. In highly industrialized countries, the middle classes tended to be liberals, the manual workers socialists; both thought in terms of progress and had no use for a church that was devoted to conservative interests. The rise of industrialization was accompanied, therefore, by a massive de-Christianization of Western Europe.

If this process was to be reversed, or even arrested, something clearly would have to be done. What was needed was a new and much more independent line of Catholic political action, one that would appeal to something more than the traditional faith of rural conservatives. If the church was to survive in the modern world, it would have to show that its eternal Christian truths were relevant to the changing needs of an urban and industrial society. To break loose from traditional conservatism was a matter of life or death.

LEO XIII AND THE REORIENTATION
OF CATHOLIC POLITICAL THOUGHT

The man who did the most to effect this painful reorientation, and to direct the church toward more effective lines of political and social action, was Pope Leo XIII. His unusually long pontificate, from 1878 to 1903, coincided with one of the most critical periods in the history of the papacy. When he came to the throne, the political fortunes of the modern church had reached their lowest ebb. From a Catholic standpoint, 1870 had been a year of unparalleled disaster. Rome, the last vestige of the former Papal States, had been annexed by the Kingdom of Italy, and for more than fifty years thereafter the popes of Rome, as self-styled "Prisoners of the Vatican," were destined to remain in an attitude of uncompromising hostility toward the government of Rome itself. As if this were not enough, the same year also brought developments that decisively weakened the Catholic position in France and Germany. The Franco-Prussian War led to the overthrow of the pro-Catholic French Empire, and to the establishment of a Third Republic that became, in the course of time, bitterly anticlerical. It also led to the absorption of many Catholic states in a Protestant German Empire that soon embarked on a strenuous though ultimately unsuccessful policy of trying to force all German Catholics to break their ties with Rome. Leo XIII was the first pope who, therefore, had to face squarely up to the problem of running the church under typically modern conditions. No longer willing to play their traditional role in a Christian commonwealth, most of the political authorities with whom he had to deal were hostile or, at best, indifferent, to Catholic teachings. Under these trying conditions he had to seek new forms of Catholic action. His success marks him as the first, and perhaps the greatest, of the popes of the modern church.

Pope Leo's political and social views were published, along with other matters, in a remarkable series of papal encyclicals. An encyclical is a letter addressed to the world at large on matters of general interest. As an official pronouncement of the Holy See, it is something less, and something more, than an expression of the pope's own personal opinions. It is prepared after long and serious consultation with other leading members of the hierarchy and speaks with the authority of an ancient and

continuing Catholic tradition. Within the framework of Catholic orthodoxy, however, there are many permissible variations of thought and
emphasis. As the acknowledged and sovereign head of the church, each
pope in turn bears final responsibility for the choice among many different lines of possible future development. Pope Leo himself was especially
devoted to the works of St. Thomas Aquinas. Of all the leading schools
of Catholic orthodoxy, Thomism is the one that goes farthest in its
emphasis on the power of human reason. As compared with those who
lay greater stress on the mystical aspects of Christianity, good Thomists
are particularly disposed to work for the achievement of Christian goals
by political and social means. Pope Leo shared this point of view and
encouraged its development. In one of his earlier encyclicals, the *Aeternam
Patris,* he officially acclaimed Aquinas as the most reliable and authoritative of all the fathers of the church. His own approach to the problems
of contemporary society was essentially Thomist in character.

Christian Socialism

From a political standpoint, one of the most notable features of Leo's
pontificate was his success in encouraging a new and vigorous movement,
often known as "Christian socialism." This movement received its official
justification in *Rerum Novarum,* the first of a long series of encyclicals that
have helped to define the attitude of the modern church on social and
political questions. For some time past, conscientious members of the
church had been much disturbed by the steady worsening of class relations in modern industrial societies. From a Catholic standpoint, employers and workers were equally to blame. In a truly rational society, all
economic relations would be conducted in a spirit of mutual consideration and regulated by a common sense of social justice. Both natural
reason and Christian truth require all men and women to regard one
another as brothers and sisters engaged in a common enterprise. Hateful
and wrongheaded ideologies had served of late to destroy this normal
relationship. Liberalism had taught employers to be completely selfish,
using their economic power to drive down wages and other conditions
of employment to the lowest possible point. Socialism, in return, had
taught the workers to be envious and resentful of the rich, denying them
their natural right to private property. The only way out of this impasse
was to return to basic principles of social justice. Workers and employers
should come together, under Catholic auspices, in mutually beneficial
associations in which each would learn to respect the just needs and
welfare of the other. These were the principles that Leo advocated as a
Catholic solution to the modern "social question."

Although Catholic socialism had some success, its ultimate value
was political rather than economic. It is true that a number of trade
unions and workers' cooperatives were established in accordance with

Catholic principles, and that many employers were effectively moved by the call to social justice. By the end of the nineteenth century the new movement had already become an appreciable factor in the field of industrial relations. Neither then nor thereafter was it able, however, to rival Marxism as a preponderant influence in the lives of the proletariat. Its main significance was to provide a useful nucleus of working-class support for Catholic political parties. Such parties proved, in the course of time, to be the most effective vehicles of Catholic social action.

The Problem of Liberal Democracy

Unfortunately there were still many theoretical and emotional objections to be overcome before the Catholics could make full use of their political opportunities. The difficulty was that, from 1870 onward, most European countries were committed to liberal principles of government. Though few as yet were republics, the standard form of modern kingship was constitutional monarchy, increasingly democratic in character, which was content to exercise authority on a basis of popular consent. Many of the new regimes had been set up, moreover, by revolutionary means. From the standpoint of traditional Catholicism, all this was unacceptable. For generations the church had been teaching that the power of kings was ordained by God and that revolution was a sin. How, then, could Catholics participate in popular governments without condoning sin? How, above all, could they participate in liberal governments without abandoning their most sacred principles? The only proper form of government was one where the principles of Catholic morality were enforced by public authority, and where the exercise of civil and political liberties was restricted to members of the Catholic Church. This was no arbitrary and indifferent thing, but a natural consequence of the Catholic principle that the public has a right to be protected against pernicious errors, and that the church, in all questions related to faith and morals, has been ordained by God himself as the final judge of truth. To accept a liberal constitution, which guaranteed freedom of speech and religion to all, would seem to be nothing less than a surrender of the church's claim to divine infallibility.

It is a measure of Leo's greatness that he saw the need of overcoming these objections. This does not mean that he rejected the validity of the church's earlier position. Like his master, Aquinas, he believed that monarchy is the most natural type of government, that it is sinful to rebel against legitimate authorities, and that the Christian commonwealth is the best form of society. His encyclicals continued to teach these basic truths and to anathematize the liberal conception of freedom. He recognized, however, that it would be fatal for Catholics to abstain from political action. He therefore took care to emphasize those aspects of the Catholic tradition that could be used to justify participation.

Theoretical Bases for Catholic Collaboration

Objections to democracy, as such, were easy to refute. Although Catholic theologians had often expressed a preference for monarchy, on the ground that it reflected the natural order of things in a universe ruled monarchically by God, they had always recognized that aristocracy and democracy, too, were legitimate forms of government. In the Catholic Middle Ages there had been many republics, and a few of them, most notably Switzerland, had survived to modern times. Such regimes had always been perfectly acceptable from the standpoint of the Catholic Church. It is true that all power is ordained by God, and receives its legitimacy from Him. There is no reason, however, why one of the legitimate means of transmitting this power should not be by popular action, as well as by hereditary succession. Popular governments, under proper Catholic guidance, are entirely capable of living up to the requirements of a Christian commonwealth. The authority of such governments had never been questioned by any right-thinking Catholic.

Liberal and revolutionary democracies were a different story, but even here the difficulties were not insuperable. The church, after all, had always had to face the fact that Catholics cannot necessarily expect to enjoy the privilege of living in a Christian commonwealth. Many, like the Christians of ancient Rome, had been subject to pagan rulers; others had been subject to heretics. Even in the heyday of absolute monarchy, there had been substantial Catholic minorities in many Protestant states. As powers that be, pagan and heretical rulers are also ordained by God, in His inscrutable wisdom, and ought to be obeyed. Because of its adherence to this principle, the church had regularly refrained from sanctioning any sort of rebellion against the liberal and revolutionary governments of nineteenth-century Europe. But if Catholics owe a duty of allegiance to constitutional democracies, why should they not also make use of opportunities for democratic action to further the interests of the church and to press, as far as possible, for the adoption of Catholic policies? In countries like the United States, where the Catholics had always been in the minority, the church had never doubted the wisdom of encouraging its members to participate fully in the political life of the community, even though this meant cooperating with Protestants. In most European countries, the situation of the Catholics was essentially similar to that of their American co-religionists. It was hard to avoid the conclusion that their political policy likewise ought to be the same.

The Heritage of Leo XIII

Though Leo, in practice, was clearly reluctant to follow this line, he adopted it in principle. His reluctance is understandable. To begin with, the idea of taking part in the politics of democracy was bound to be much

64

more distasteful to European Catholics, long devoted to conservative traditions, than to democratic-minded Americans. The bitter anticlerical and anti-Christian sentiments of European liberals and socialists also made it harder for them than for most non-Catholic Americans to cooperate with loyal members of the church. Pope Leo's own encyclicals did nothing to appease that hostility. In spite of all difficulties, however, the sheer necessities of the situation made it necessary for him to broaden the basis of Catholic action. Because of the Roman question, his opposition to the Italian government remained uncompromising, and Italian Catholics were forbidden, to the end of his pontificate and beyond, to participate in Italian politics. When the German Empire, on the other hand, persisted in attacking the Catholic Church, he encouraged the formation of a Catholic party to defend church interests by parliamentary means. More striking still was the attempt he made, in 1889, to rally French Catholics to the cause of the French Republic, urging them to abandon their uncompromising monarchism, and to accept the new regime as a legitimate basis for political action. This event, alone, was enough to mark the beginning of a new era in Catholic politics.

What Leo XIII managed to do, in the course of his long pontificate, was to lay the groundwork for what proved to be the church's most effective line of approach to the problems of modern society. The Age of Ideology has been a dangerous period in the history of Christianity. Its prevailing currents of thought have been basically at variance with the Christian point of view. In matters of doctrine the Catholic church has been willing to make no concessions. It has continued to teach truths which it still regards as eternal and unchanging. In matters of politics, on the other hand, it has shown considerable flexibility. Without abandoning its ideal of the Christian commonwealth as an ultimate objective, it has accepted the necessity of working in a world which is by no means preponderantly Christian. In Western Europe this has often led, as in the case of Weimar Germany, to the formation of Catholic parties that are willing to collaborate with liberals and socialists in support of constitutional democracy. This is a far cry from the inflexible conservatism of the church's former position. By giving their own organizations the broadest possible base, and by negotiating freely with other groups for the attainment of desirable objectives, it has been possible for Catholic minorities to make themselves felt as a substantial force in the Age of Ideology. Their success stems directly from the social and political doctrines of the man who presided over the destiny of the Catholic Church at the end of the nineteenth century.

CHAPTER NINE

SOCIAL DEMOCRACY

Of the three main groups associated in the Weimar coalition of 1918, the largest and most surprising was the Social Democratic party. Liberals and Catholics had long since abandoned their former intransigence and accepted the necessity of negotiating their differences. In joining forces to establish a constitutional democracy they, at least, were on familiar ground. For the German Social Democrats, on the other hand, it was a different story. Theirs had been, for some time past, the largest and most successful of socialist movements. The party's commitment to revolutionary Marxism had recently been reaffirmed, moreover, after heated controversy with a more moderate group known as the "revisionists." When the loss of World War I led to the collapse of the German Empire, they might well have been expected to try to redeem their revolutionary promises. A small minority did in fact attempt to follow the lead of the Russian communists, who had just given the world its first example of a successful proletarian revolution. But in spite of all this, the Social Democrats adopted a different course. Instead of trying to seize power on their own account, they threw the whole weight of their authority on the side of constitutional democracy. In close collaboration with non-Marxist parties, they played a decisive part in the establishment and defense of the Weimar Republic. When revolutionary Marxists tried to overthrow the new regime, it was a Social Democratic minister of the interior, serving under a Social Democratic president, who assumed responsibility for crushing the rebellion. A good deal of water had gone over the dam since the days of Marx and Engels.

THE FATE OF ORTHODOX MARXISM

After studying the earlier phases of the Industrial Revolution, Marx had concluded that the economic power of the capitalists was growing steadily weaker, but that their political power would remain intact until it was finally overthrown by a proletarian revolution. As things turned out, it was the political power of the capitalists that tended to decline, while their position in the economy remained unshaken. Since the predicted collapse of capitalism did not take place, socialists found in practice that their hoped-for revolution would have to be deferred. They also discovered, on the other hand, that a capitalist society provided the working classes with occasional unexpected opportunities for effective political action. To make use of these opportunities without abandoning the Marxist ideology has been the typical dilemma of modern socialism.

One weak point of the Marxian dialectic was its underestimate of the productivity and resourcefulness of the capitalist system of production. Its theory had rested on the proposition that the world of modern industry would consist of an ever smaller and richer capitalist class exploiting an ever larger and more impoverished proletariat. Although the earlier stages of the Industrial Revolution seemed to point in this direction, its later development was quite different. As the Industrial Revolution progressed, the number of capitalists tended not to shrink but to increase. The number of factory workers also increased, but never to the point of becoming a majority of the total population. The complex process of modern industry called for the services of an ever larger army of managers, technicians, and other salaried employees who stubbornly refused to regard themselves as proletarians. The productive capacity of the new industrial economy was so great, moreover, that it was possible to satisfy the expectations of owners and white-collar workers without forcing the wages of day-laborers down to the starvation level that Marx had predicted.

THE EFFECTS OF TRADE UNIONISM

One of the reasons for this situation was the growth of the trade union movement. Marx's failure to recognize the true significance of this development was a consequence of his general tendency to overestimate the political power of capitalism. In the earlier days of the Industrial Revolution, trade unions had generally been prohibited by law, as conspiracies in restraint of trade. Marx assumed that as long as capitalism lasted, the bourgeois state would continue to prevent workers from combining in defense of their economic interests and that employers would therefore enjoy a decisive advantage in bargaining with workers. The power of governments proved insufficient, however, to prevent industrial workers from organizing. The final result was abandonment of the capitalist position and a general recognition of the right to collective bargaining. This was a decisive demonstration of the political power of the workers and of their ability to force concessions from the ruling class.

As leaders of the proletariat, the socialists generally welcomed and supported this development. They could do so, without prejudice to their Marxist theories, on the assumption that trade-union activities could never take the place of, but would simply prepare the way for, the inevitable revolution. In their opinion, the inherent weaknesses of capitalism were such that the employers could make no concessions to the demands of their workers without undermining their own economic power, which depended on profits derived exclusively from the exploitation of labor. Since this was so, there could be no hope of improving the lot of the working classes by trade-union action. Trade unions could still perform a useful function, however. By participating in strikes and other acts of industrial warfare, organized workers would learn to recognize capitalists as their natural enemies, becoming in the process full-fledged revolutionary members of the class-conscious proletariat. By making their employers lose money, they would also weaken the economic power of capitalism and hasten its demise. The value of unionism seemed quite clear from the standpoint of orthodox Marxism.

NEW OPPORTUNITIES
FOR POLITICAL ACTION

As things turned out, the effect of trade unions was quite different. It is true that strikes and other organized activities did serve, as expected, to increase the class-consciousness of the proletariat. The political strength of the socialist movement gained much from its trade-union members; its revolutionary potential did not. The trouble was that collective bargaining was generally successful. Though they resisted as long as possible, employers for the most part were capable of making substantial concessions without going out of business. The net effect of trade-union action was not to weaken the economic power of the capitalists, but to improve the standard of living of the workers. As their economic position improved, the latter tended to become more interested in immediate opportunities for bargaining than in distant revolutionary hopes. Without abandoning the rhetoric of class warfare, they grew used to the ways of peaceful negotiation.

Changes in the character of European politics also worked in the same direction. In the days when Marx had been developing his theories, it had seemed only natural to suppose that the state was a bourgeois institution. Before 1870, the proletariat had had very few opportunities for legitimate political action. Most powers still rested in the hands of kings, and the right to vote was generally restricted to men of property. Under these circumstances revolution might well seem to be the only political resource available to the proletariat. From 1870 onward, the situation changed. National legislatures based on universal male suffrage were set up in many countries, including the new German Empire, and their powers were much increased. Any group with a sizable popular following could now aspire to legitimate political power. The socialists, with their solid basis of support among well-organized trade unionists, were in a position to profit greatly from the rise of political democracy. Once again they were offered a possible alternative to revolutionary action.

THE RELUCTANCE OF MARXISTS
TO SUBSTITUTE POLITICAL FOR REVOLUTIONARY ACTION

In this case the Marxists were clearly reluctant to make full use of their powers. To participate in a strictly working-class organization, the trade union, was one thing; to compete for seats in a bourgeois parliament was something else again. Like industrial warfare, electoral competition might well prove useful in stimulating class-consciousness and in testing the strength of proletarian forces. It was generally agreed, therefore, that Marxists ought to take the lead in establishing socialist parties and in working for the election of socialist candidates wherever possible. This they did, with much success. By the end of the century, the Social Democrats had already become the largest and best-disciplined party in the German Reichstag. The real issue was how the socialists ought to make use of their parliamentary representatives. Socialist deputies certainly ought to avail themselves of every opportunity to make known their own position and to obstruct the work of their middle-class enemies. Should they also try to attack the established system more directly by trying to secure the enactment of socialist legislation? This would, if successful, have the useful effect of weakening the capitalist economy. Since the socialists were a minority, on the other hand, the only way of achieving this would be to cooperate with other parties. Could this be done without compromising the revolutionary character of the movement? Orthodox Marxists found it hard to agree on the answer to this question.

The immediate advantages of cooperation were so great, however, that it was hard to resist them just for the sake of remote revolutionary objectives. The prestige of socialism was now involved in electoral failures and successes. To risk losing votes by unpopular actions was no light thing. Accustomed to the give and take of industrial negotiations, trade unionists would be likely to appreciate the desirability of good political bargains and to grow impatient with theoretical purists who tried to stand in their way. The result was constant pressure on the side of collaboration. Socialist parties soon grew into the habit of supporting specific measures that seemed, though inadequate from a strictly Marxist standpoint, to stand some chance of making improvements in the lot of the working classes. When a relatively favorable government was threatened, moreover, with a vote of no-confidence which might lead to its replacement by one less favorable, they often found it necessary to lend these governments their votes, or at least to abstain from voting with the opposition.

To assume direct responsibility by participating with other parties in a coalition cabinet was a final step that they long refused to take. At the turn of the century, the French socialists still insisted that any deputy who became a cabinet minister was a traitor to the party, subject to expulsion. Such purism, however, was out of date and had to be abandoned. From the moment when European socialists first decided to participate in democratic elections, there was no resisting the pressure that forced them, in the end, to take a full and responsible part in the processes of constitutional democracy.

NEW OPPORTUNITIES FOR COLLABORATION
WITH NON-MARXIST PARTIES

This outcome was greatly facilitated, moreover, by parallel developments which had also been taking place in the non-Marxist camp. If liberals and conservatives had continued their earlier intransigence, it would have been hard for the socialists, with the best will in the world, to find an acceptable basis for cooperating with them. This was not the case. Ever since the days of John Stuart Mill, middle-class parties had been growing ever less rigid in their adherence to the ideology of liberalism. Conservatives too, including the Catholics, were disposed to take an increasingly flexible view of the need for changes in the old established order. By the end of the nineteenth century many people had come to regard human welfare as the ultimate criterion of political and social action, and to recognize wide-ranging experiment and compromise as proper means of achieving their objectives. Many liberals, like the Englishman, T. H. Green, without abandoning their preference for free enterprise, were prepared to go much further than Mill in accepting the need for wages-and-hours laws, social insurance, and other forms of government intervention to correct certain undesirable consequences of free competition. The Catholics, with their emphasis on social justice, were still better disposed toward modern forms of social legislation. Although many sharp divisions of opinion still remained, there were many possible grounds for agreement with the exponents of modern socialism.

An essential factor in all these developments was the steady increase of humanitarian sentiments. This is well illustrated by the career of Jean Jaurès, the most popular exponent of French socialism in the period immediately preceding World War I. Jaurès was an outstandingly gifted professor of philosophy, who began his parliamentary career as a representative of middle-class republicanism. From the very start, however, his main interest in politics had been motivated by a strong humanitarian concern for the plight of the working classes. He came from a comparatively backward district in the south of France. Life there had been dominated for generations by an extremely rich and ruthless family, who had used its control over the local mines and industries to hold down the wages and control the votes of the working-class population. Jaurès, as a philosophical humanist, felt that the poverty and subservience of these people was a violation of the most elementary requirements of human dignity. Sympathetic with the efforts of socialist trade unions to win their independence, he soon became a socialist himself. However, he naturally tended to emphasize the idealistic and humanitarian aspects of Marxism, and to think of socialism as a defense of a human being's natural right to freedom and self-development. His broad and generous position, unlike the more rigorous materialism of the more orthodox Marxists, was capable of making a strong appeal to the moral sense of many non-Marxists. Through his influence, it became much easier than before to mobilize the humanitarianism of other parties in support of socialist objectives.

THE NEED FOR A REVISION
OF ORTHODOX MARXISM

One obstacle, however, still stood in the way of collaboration between Marxists and non-Marxists: the ideology of Marxism itself. From the very beginning, the new doctrine had owed most of its appeal to its promise of total revolution. Socialists had been taught to view the world in terms of black and white. Against the total injustice of capitalism, they were the prophets of a totally just new order that could be brought into existence by nothing less than a total revolution. This was an inspiring faith, not easily abandoned. Jaurès himself, though he went much farther than most in recognizing the need for parliamentary action, was never willing to abandon the idea that the goal of socialism was to destroy capitalism completely, and that revolutionary violence might well be necessary for the final accomplishment of that purpose. As long as the socialists remained fully committed to this ideology, it would obviously be hard for them to work together with non-socialists in an atmosphere of mutual confidence and respect.

At the turn of the century there emerged a group of socialists, known as the Revisionists, who made a serious attempt to overcome this difficulty. The leader of this group was Eduard Bernstein. Though a German, he had spent many years in England, and had been much influenced by the British point of view. Socialist ideas had made a good deal of headway there by the end of the nineteenth century. The strength of the British parliamentary tradition was such, however, that British socialism had always remained relatively immune to the appeals of revolutionary Marxism. The most influential group there were the Fabians, who had absorbed many Marxist ideas but believed in the possibility of reforming capitalistic society by parliamentary action. Socialism would replace capitalism, the Fabians argued, not by revolution, but through the gradual and inevitable evolutionary transformation of the economy into collectivist patterns. Bernstein agreed with them, and in 1901 he published a book, *Evolutionary Socialism*, which tried to show his continental colleagues the error of their ways. By an impressive marshaling of statistical facts, he proved that Marx had been essentially wrong in his predictions about the development of modern capitalism. He pointed out that the proletariat were not, in fact, growing more numerous or more impoverished in the course of time, but that their opportunities for effective parliamentary action were steadily increasing. He therefore urged that the socialists "revise" their outworn revolutionary Marxism, and make full use of their actual political strength. He insisted that socialism could be achieved through parliamentary politics and democratic methods. Marx was right about the inevitability of socialism, but wrong in believing that only revolution could bring it about. The argument of Bernstein's book would become gospel for generations of European and American social democrats.

THE FATE OF REVISIONISM

Although the Revisionism of the Fabians and Bernstein was widely discussed in socialist circles, the reaction to it was generally unfavorable. The Germans, in particular, were unwilling to deviate from Marxist orthodoxy, and regarded Bernstein as no less than a traitor to the cause of the proletariat. Revolutionary Marxism had won them a vast and faithful following among the German working classes. True to the revolutionary tradition, the leaders of German socialism threw the whole weight of their prestige, both at home and abroad, against the Revisionist movement. The effect of Bernstein's efforts was not to shake but, on the whole, to confirm and strengthen the influence of the original ideology. Only in

1914, with the outbreak of World War I, would one of the major short-comings of revolutionary socialism first manifest itself. Nationalism, rather than Revisionism, would be the rock on which it foundered.

One of the prime articles of the Marxist creed had always been its uncompromising rejection of the nationalist movement. Nations, so the theory went, were a strictly bourgeois affair. Although capitalists might do their best to divide the toiling masses by fomenting national antago-nisms, no properly class-conscious proletarian would fail to recognize that exploited workers have no fatherland, but owe allegiance to the world proletariat. Any declaration of war between advanced industrial states should be taken, therefore, as a signal for socialists on both sides of the border to join hands and overthrow their respective governments.

World War I, which involved all the leading powers of Europe, provided the first decisive occasion for putting these theories into prac-tice. The result was to show that nationalism, even among the class conscious proletariat, was an unexpectedly powerful force. In the days when peace hung in the balance, many socialist leaders, most notably Jaurès, made valiant efforts to throw the weight of international socialism against the threat of war. The result was negligible. In the face of an irresistible upsurge of national sentiments, most socialists soon found good reasons for supporting the war effort. The behavior of the Ger-mans, who had so recently taken the lead in condemning Revisionism, was especially remarkable. All but two of the large socialist delegation in the Reichstag promptly joined their bourgeois colleagues in voting for the huge war credits required by the Germany army. The record of socialist leaders in other countries was very much the same. Jaurès never had to face the issue; he was assassinated by a fanatical French nationalist just as the war began. But French socialists, in general, proved quite as patriotic as their German brothers. The war, long awaited as an opportu-nity for workers of the world to unite against their own national govern-ments, served rather to give them new occasions for cooperating with other classes in defense of their respective nations.

This event marks the decisive turning point in the history of modern socialism. A minority, who refused to abandon the promise of revolution-ary Marxism, found it necessary to break with the established socialist parties. They generally wound up as communists. The majority, however, having once accepted the responsibility of cooperating with non-socialist parties, found it hard to justify any real return to their former intransi-gence. When the war they had supported was lost, the German socialists had no choice, as patriotic Germans, but to join with other parties in the attempt to establish a new regime of constitutional democracy, even if this meant suppressing the new minority of revolutionary Marxists. Con-trary to former precedents, they had to accept positions of responsibility in governments that fell far short of being strictly socialistic. Although they had rejected Revisionism in theory, Revisionism in fact was the policy to which the logic of events had brought them. The ideology of Marxism was no longer strong enough to keep them from full-fledged participation in the process of constitutional government. This has proved to be the typical line of development in twentieth-century social-ism.

CHAPTER TEN

COMMUNISM

When the German socialists fought against their own revolutionary minority in defense of the Weimar Republic, their decision was important not only for its immediate significance but as a sign of things to come. Many people thought of it, at the time, as no more than a local skirmish; actually it was the first major engagement in the conflict between revolutionary Marxism and liberal democracy. By accepting the principles of constitutional government, the majority socialists joined with other groups in supporting a parliamentary system based on party competition. The minority socialists, on the contrary, were inspired by a very different model. Just before the end of World War I, revolutionary Marxists had succeeded in overthrowing the government of Tsarist Russia. In its place they were setting up a "dictatorship of the proletariat," a new kind of regime based on the revolutionary power of a small, well-organized elite, the Communist party. Though communism failed in Germany, its success in Russia was to provide the basis for many future experiments in government by revolutionary minorities.

THE CONDITION OF TSARIST RUSSIA

Although attempts to Westernize Russia had been going on for more than two centuries, since the days of Peter the Great, the process was still far from complete. Russia had made itself strong enough to retain its independence, like Japan, and even to play the role of a great power in world politics. During the past century it had also begun to produce men like Tolstoy and Mendeleev whose literary and scientific contributions to

Western civilization were recognized as second to none. In spite of all this, however, Russia was still a backward country. It had little in the way of modern industry, and much of what it had was controlled by foreign capitalists and technicians. The great majority of the population were backward and illiterate peasants whose way of life had been largely untouched by Western civilization. This peasant mass had little in common with the Westernized upper classes. Political authority was exercised by a Tsarist government as autocratic and exempt from popular controls as any colonial administration. All in all, Russia still had a long way to go before it could rank with other Western nations.

Politically speaking, the most important consequence of this situation was a steady increase of revolutionary sentiment. Although several Tsars had taken a leading part in the attempt to modernize Russia, their willingness to sanction radical changes was limited by the fact that their own authority as autocrats was based on old traditions, and was bound to suffer with the introduction of modern ways of thought. As modernization proceeded, they tended, therefore, to become increasingly suspicious of the more progressive Russians and to entrust the affairs of the country to conservative aristocrats. This placed them in a hopeless position. The Tsarist regime was not conservative enough to arrest the decay of traditional Russia and thus to retain the allegiance of the more traditional classes of the population; it was far too conservative, on the other hand, to satisfy the modernists. When the latter compared their country with Western nations, they found it greatly wanting. Dissatisfaction became especially acute after the Russo-Japanese war of 1903, when the newly modernized Japanese Empire proved decisively superior to Russia in the use of contemporary military techniques. This alienated progressive Russians from the discredited Tsarist regime and made them increasingly susceptible to thoughts of revolution.

MARXISM IN RUSSIA

In the climate of opinion then prevailing, it was natural for nineteenth-century Russians to look to the West for enlightenment. When Marxism emerged as the newest form of European radicalism, it was eagerly grasped by many as an answer to their problems. The works of Marx and Engels were translated into Russian almost as soon as they were written, and, in spite of Tsarist censorship, achieved wide circulation. A number of Russians became early converts to revolutionary Marxism. They played a minor but increasingly important part in the development of the prewar socialist movement.

Unfortunately, Marxism, from a Russian standpoint, was a rather discouraging doctrine. Its hopes for the future were all based on condi-

tions that were supposed to emerge in the later stages of modern indus-
trialism. Marx had started from the assumption that a fully developed
capitalist society was already in existence. His confidence in the coming
revolution depended on his belief that capitalism itself would produce a
class of factory workers so much larger than any other class that it would
ultimately be able to overwhelm its capitalist rulers by sheer weight of
numbers. None of this applied to prewar Russia, which was still in a
precapitalist stage of development. A nation of peasants and landlords,
it had only a small minority of factory workers, and its even smaller
minority of capitalists was very far from constituting a ruling class. According to the principles of the dialectic, it would seem, therefore, that
a long period of capitalist development would be needed before there
could be any hope of proletarian revolution. To anyone who longed for
a classless society, this was a dreary prospect.

LENIN'S INVENTION: THE REVOLUTIONARY PARTY

Lenin, the future leader of the Russian Revolution, was a revolutionary
Marxist who refused to accept this conclusion. As a thoroughly Westernized middle-class intellectual, he had devoted his life to the destruction
of the established order, and was bitterly opposed to anything that might
compromise his revolutionary hopes. His own talent, as events were to
show, was for skillful political action. His shrewd political sense told him,
moreover, that a revolutionary crisis could not be long delayed. The
Russian proletariat was weak, to be sure, but the capitalists they con-
fronted were even weaker. The real key to the situation lay, however, in
the decline of the Russian state. After decades of inefficient despotism,
the Tsarist regime was rapidly discouraging or alienating the last of its
supporters. To overthrow so flimsy a structure, weak forces would suffice.
If a small but devoted minority was prepared for revolutionary action, it
might soon find a favorable opportunity to overthrow the government.
In a country long unaccustomed to responsible political action, the result
would be a period of complete confusion. Under these conditions a
revolutionary minority, as the only well-organized and decisive group in
the community, might well be able to control the situation, for a time, at
least. To prepare for such an eventuality was, in Lenin's view, the mission
of Russian Marxism.

By following this line of thought, Lenin became the inventor of a
wholly new type of political organization, the revolutionary party. The
formation of political parties had long been recognized as an indispensable means of mobilizing mass electorates. In Western Europe, socialist
parties with a million or more followers were already in existence. In
Russia, where the proletariat was small, and where all forms of political

organization were ruthlessly suppressed, there was no real hope of building up a mass party of this sort. Lenin's most original contribution to the art of politics lay in his recognition of the fact that the cause of revolution would be better served by a quite different kind of organization. In one of his more notable early writings, *What Is to Be Done,* he laid down the specifications for a new and truly revolutionary type of political party. Size in this case was not to be a primary consideration. Instead of trying to include all and sundry, the Communist party should be rigorously exclusive. It should consist of a hard core of professional revolutionaries, undeviating in their loyalty to the party program. The function of this well-disciplined elite would be to infiltrate and gain positions of leadership in more popular organizations, using them as "transmission belts" for the exercise of power. In this way a small nucleus of party members would be able to control the activities of a vastly larger number of outsiders and use them for revolutionary purposes. This was the theory that Lenin, as a man of action, proceeded to apply in practice. Under his skilled leadership, the Communist party of Russia became the first example of a modern revolutionary party.

THE PROBLEM OF RECONCILING
LENINISM WITH ORTHODOX MARXISM

In relying on a highly disciplined party elite for the accomplishment of revolutionary purposes, Lenin was clearly opposed to the current trend toward democratic socialism. The ambiguities of Marx's own attitude toward democracy were such, however, that it was possible for communists to defend their position in terms of orthodox Marxism. Though Marx and Engels, as we have seen, generally spoke of the coming revolution as a democratic movement, they had occasionally used the word "dictatorship" to characterize the ensuing proletarian regime, and had also made use of phrases like "class-conscious proletariat" and "vanguard of the proletariat," that seemed to suggest an elitist view of the revolutionary process. These aspects of the earlier doctrine were seized on and amplified by Lenin and his successors. Identifying their own party of professional revolutionaries as the true vanguard of the proletariat, the Russian communists claimed that they alone, as the most advanced and class-conscious sector of the proletariat, had an exclusive right to act as spokesmen for the proletariat as a whole and to exercise the dictatorial powers of the proletariat over the rest of society. According to this new version of Marxism, it was no longer relevant to ask whether the proletariat had the support of a majority of the population, or even whether the party had achieved democratic leadership within the proletariat itself. All that mattered was that a properly qualified revolutionary elite should come into power, and use that power to establish effective revolutionary authority on behalf of the proletariat.

From the standpoint of orthodox Marxism, however, an awkward question still remained to be answered. The basic principle of "scientific socialism," the principle that distinguished it from mere utopianism, was its dialectical materialism. Belief in the inevitability of a proletarian revolution, and in the emergence of a perfect classless society, had always rested on the supposed pre-existence of a fully developed capitalist economy. Since Tsarist Russia was still in a distinctly precapitalist stage of development, the obvious conclusion would seem to be that the time was not yet ripe for a proletarian revolution in that country. How, then, could Russian Marxists engage in revolutionary activities without doing violence to one of the essential tenets of their own ideology?

The Theory of Imperialism

Lenin's *Imperialism* was an attempt to answer this question. In the decades preceding World War I, the most highly developed industrial nations of Western Europe had been engaged in a bitterly competitive attempt to extend their respective colonial empires. Analyzing these developments in Marxist terms, Lenin concluded that this was a typical symptom of capitalist decay. Unable to find home markets for their ever-expanding production, advanced industrial countries had been able to keep going for the time being by seizing colonial markets. By exploiting the surplus value of colonial labor, Western capitalists had even succeeded in operating at a profit without fully exploiting their own domestic laboring forces. This had enabled them, contrary to Marx' original prediction, to expand without forcing the wages of their workers down to the level of subsistence. By "exporting poverty abroad" they had managed to keep the European proletariat relatively prosperous, thus delaying the development of a true proletarian class consciousness in the more advanced industrial nations. All this depended, however, on the continuous acquisition of fresh colonial markets. Since the area of possible imperial expansion was strictly limited, the process could not long continue. This meant that the final stage of capitalism would inevitably assume the form of imperialist warfare, as rival empires engaged in a hopeless struggle to the death for the control of dwindling colonial markets. According to Lenin, the outbreak of World War I was proof that this stage had at last been reached, and that the capitalist system, now fully matured, was ripe for dissolution.

Under these conditions, it was possible to find a new basis for the justification of revolutionary activities in economically backward regions. Although relatively unindustrialized countries like Tsarist Russia were not themselves capitalist, they were indispensable, as markets and as suppliers of cheap raw materials, to the continuation of Western capitalism. A political revolution that succeeded in depriving the West of its ability to control and exploit these regions would destroy the whole system. Because of their economic backwardness, moreover, the inhabitants of these regions had long been the most cruelly exploited of all the world's workers, and were therefore an especially promising field for revolutionary agitation. From this Lenin concluded that the disintegration of capitalism would begin not in the industrial heartland but at the colonial periphery of the capitalist world. Because of the peculiar weakness of the Tsarist political system, Russia might well be the country which, by offering the first effective challenge to capitalist imperialism, was destined to become the starting point of a worldwide revolution. This was Lenin's justification for the establishment of a party of professional revolutionaries in his own native land.

THE REVOLUTION OF 1917

The accuracy of the Russian leader's predictions was very soon put to the test. As far as Russia itself was concerned, his hopes were fully justified. Unable to cope with the disastrous events of World War I, the long outmoded Tsarist government was finally overthrown. The chaos that followed provided the communists with ample opportunity to demonstrate their skill as professional revolutionaries. Although the party, at the outset, amounted to no more than a tiny fraction of the total population, their incomparable discipline, and their skillful use of transmission-belt tactics, ultimately enabled them to overcome all rivals and to emerge as the unchallenged rulers of Russia. Successful as Lenin had been, however, as a prophet of events in his own country, his wider expectations were sadly disappointed. The Russian Revolution, which was supposed to inaugurate a world revolution, did nothing of the sort. In defiance of Lenin's predictions, the capitalist democracies and the colonial empires of the Western world all managed to weather the shock of war and revolution. Communism had succeeded in Russia, but in Russia alone.

The result was to bring the Communist party face to face with a painful ideological dilemma. Since the establishment of a communist regime in Russia could no longer be justified as part of a worldwide communist movement, the undeveloped character of the Russian economy remained as an unresolved problem. Should the new rulers of the country, faithful to the principle of dialectical materialism, recognize that Russia was not yet ripe for communism and accept the necessity of a preliminary stage of normal capitalist growth? Logical and necessary as this might seem to be from the standpoint of pure theory, it would be hard in practice for a militantly anticapitalist movement to accept so self-effacing a policy. Or should the party take advantage of its political position, and use the power of the state to inaugurate a program of economic development? This might be desirable, but it would involve a strange reversal of the Marxist principle that economics are prior to politics. This, too, would be hard to reconcile with the principles of orthodox Marxism.

THE COMMUNIST REVISION
OF ORTHODOX MARXISM

Of the available alternatives, the latter was the one that the communists elected. Reluctantly abandoning their original hopes for an immediate world revolution, they turned to the task of creating "communism in one country." Slowly at first, under Lenin, and then more rapidly under Stalin, his successor, they turned Russia into the first fully developed example of a modern revolutionary state. The Communist party, more firmly and centrally disciplined than ever, was able to convert a backward agrarian people into a modern industrial nation through a series of Five Year Plans. Costly and inefficient as it was in many ways, the effect of this policy was to achieve a radical transformation of the Russian economy in the course of a single generation. By the ruthless use of political power, the Communist party thus accomplished much of the work that, according to the theory of dialectical materialism, ought to have appeared only as the outcome of an historically inevitable stage of capitalist growth.

This revision of the dialectic did not mean, of course, that Lenin and his successors had ceased to be Marxists. The Russians always insisted that they were the rightful heirs of Marx and Engels, and the communist movement owed much of its remarkable vigor and self-confidence to the continuation of that belief. Their efforts found inspiration in the hope of achieving a future classless society, a society in which the state would finally wither away, and all people would freely and fully share the rewards of economic abundance. Indeed, in the writings of Lenin, especially in his *State and Revolution,* the anarchist aspect of Marxism was made a good deal more explicit than it had ever been in the works of Marx and Engels. In spite of their own reliance on political power for the accomplishment of economic purposes, the communists continued to believe in the economic interpretation of history. Their painful and at times wellnigh hopeless efforts to achieve "socialism in one country" were enlivened by the assurance that the capitalist world was bound to collapse as a consequence of its own inherent economic contradictions, and that the communist world, by abolishing private ownership of the instruments of production, had discovered the indispensable clue to genuine economic progress. As Lenin and his successors have always insisted, communism derived most of its ideological power from the scientific socialism of Marx and Engels.

CHAPTER ELEVEN

FASCISM

Although World War I did not lead to the collapse of capitalism, as Lenin had predicted, it did in fact produce a dangerous crisis in the political and economic life of the Western world. War debts and reparations, and the problems of readjustment from a wartime to a peacetime economy, gave rise to perplexing issues, issues that could not be resolved readily by the use of traditional methods. Runaway inflation and business depression became the order of the day. Under the stress of economic hardships and uncertainties, political cleavages increased in depth and bitterness. To maintain consensus under such conditions was difficult indeed. Even in countries that had long been used to the ways of constitutional government, statesmen found it hard enough to retain the support of effective parliamentary majorities; in countries where democracy was less firmly established, it proved almost impossible. Cabinets rose and fell in rapid succession, without finding generally acceptable solutions to the most urgent political problems. At a time, therefore, when the need for action was particularly pressing, constitutional democracies were afflicted by a form of creeping paralysis that seemed in many cases to be incurable.

The result was to make many Europeans look with increasing favor on experiments with dictatorship. In a time that cried out for vigorous measures, constitutional government was apparently incapable of action. Under these circumstances it was easy to conclude that dictatorship was the "wave of the future," the only truly viable form of twentieth-century politics.

THE RISE OF FASCISM

The people who adopted this position are generally known as fascists. Unlike the great ideologies of the eighteenth and nineteenth centuries, fascism was not essentially an international movement. It arose more or less independently in many different countries, in response to quite different conditions. What the various fascist movements have in common, however, is the determination to enhance the power and importance of their respective peoples by dictatorial means. To all of them the enemy was constitutional democracy, a spineless and indecisive system that could only lead to death and corruption. Marxism, above all, was the fatal virus which, by manufacturing class antagonism, was sapping the vital structure of all democratic societies. The fascists offered salvation by granting total power to a well-disciplined party elite which, under the guidance of an inspired and unquestioned leader, would restore the unity of the country and lead it forward to deeds of unparalleled greatness. Thus the crippling doubts and conflicts of the present would be replaced by the glorious certainties of a brave new world.

The party that first managed to win dictatorial powers and thereby lent its name to the movement as a whole was the Fascist party of Italy. The postwar paralysis of constitutional democracy in that country had been especially acute. The party that replaced it was, in a very personal sense, the creation of a single man, Benito Mussolini. Originally a revolutionary socialist, the future "Duce" had broken with the party over the issue of Italian participation in World War I. Nationalistically unwilling to see his own country excluded from the postwar division of spoils, he had rejected the antiwar position of the orthodox Marxists and had urged Italy to join, if belatedly, on the side of the victorious Allies. When the hope of major colonial gains was disappointed by the actual postwar settlement, and when the concurrent economic depression led to an outbreak of violent industrial conflicts, he became the recognized leader of an increasing number of nationalist-minded war veterans and others who, organized as *fasci di combattimento,* or combat groups, engaged in a long series of strike-breaking and other violent forays against the revolutionary Marxists. These groups were the nucleus of the future Fascist party. In 1922, though his party was still little larger than Lenin's had been at the time of the Russian Revolution, he succeeded, by an artful combination of bluff and violence, in persuading the existing authorities that he was the only man capable of overcoming the chronic instability of Italian parliamentary life and restoring political authority. The king appointed him prime minister, at the head of a coalition cabinet. From this vantage point he soon succeeded in destroying all effective opposition and in establishing the fascists as masters of an essentially totalitarian state.

THE NATURE OF FASCISM

Perhaps as a reaction against his own earlier commitment to Marxism, Mussolini himself was at first disposed to play down the ideological aspects of the fascist movement. In the early days of the party, "action" was the watchword, and few attempts were made to spell out, in concrete terms, the nature and direction of that action. As compared with the very elaborate and compelling communist theory of salvation by world revolution, this movement offered little that could really hope to capture the imagination of men and women and inspire them to self-sacrifice. Mussolini ultimately saw that this was a mistake and tried to rectify it. The article on "Fascism" that appeared over his signature in the *Encyclopedia Italiana* was a belated attempt to provide the movement with an effective ideology. It was not very successful. Apart from the essentially negative idea of overcoming national disunity, and the patently unrealizable goal of restoring the glories of ancient Rome, Italian fascism never offered very much in the way of a vision of the future. Although domestic unity and imperial aggrandizement were ideas well-calculated to mobilize the support of existing nationalist sentiments, they were hardly new or exciting enough to generate a real revolution. The Fascist party was little more than a clique of officeholders, more interested in enjoying the spoils of absolute power than in pursuing revolutionary experiments. Not in Italy only, but in other countries as well, lack of an effective ideology was a typical and persistent weakness of the whole fascist movement.

NAZISM

The one exception was Nazism. This movement arose in Germany at about the same time, and under much the same conditions, as its Italian counterpart. Unlike Mussolini, however, the German leader, Adolf Hitler, was not a disillusioned Marxist. He was fanatically devoted to an ideology of his own, an ideology known as racism. In some respects this was the most radical and uncompromising of all revolutionary doctrines. Liberalism and Marxism, following to this extent at least in the footsteps of Christianity, had been universal faiths, offering the promise of salvation to all humanity. Nazism, on the contrary, was exclusively devoted to the cause of a master race. This called for a truly revolutionary transformation of all existing values and institutions. To the fully committed Nazi, acceptance of membership in the party meant a sharp break with the past and a life devoted to the creation of a glorious new order. The result was a barbaric totalitarian movement the likes of which the world had never seen.

The Origins of Racism

The Nazi theory of the master race was a pseudo-science assembled from a variety of sources. Oddly enough, it was in France that the superiority of German blood was first alleged as a serious political principle. In the period preceding the French Revolution, one of the arguments used by aristocrats in the defense of their special privileges was the proposition that they, as descendants of the Germanic tribesmen who had conquered Roman Gaul, were racially superior to the rest of the population. The answer was obvious. Pretending to take the historically preposterous argument at face value, antiaristocratic pamphleteers proceeded to claim, at the time of the French Revolution, that the members of the Third Estate, as descendants of the ancient Gauls, were the only genuine French, and that the aristocrats, as alien oppressors, ought to go back where they came from. Nationalism provided an effective answer to this first assertion of the racist principle.

The whole episode would no doubt have been forgotten if it had not been for the development of a new and genuine science, the science of comparative linguistics. In the late eighteenth and early nineteenth centuries, the Western fund of knowledge about other times and places was vastly increased by a series of remarkable geographical and archaeological explorations. This led, among other things, to a discovery of the unexpected fact that many of the principal languages of Europe and Asia were more or less closely related, which meant that they must have descended from a single common source. As a matter of convenience, "Aryan" was a term used by many linguists to designate the unknown people who must once have spoken the original Indo-European language.

It was not long before these scientific facts, in themselves politically neutral, were combined with the earlier notions of racial superiority to produce a new and politically explosive pseudo-science. The man who first effected this mixture was a French aristocrat, the Count de Gobineau. Starting from the highly dubious assumption that the speakers of related languages must also be racially akin, he concluded that the Aryans, whose descendants had imposed their languages on so many different peoples, must have been a uniquely gifted master race. This led him to develop a philosophy of history that differed from its liberal and socialist predecessors by identifying human biology as the decisive factor in the rise and fall of civilizations. Civilization began when Aryan tribes, blond and blue-eyed, came down from the north to impose themselves as a ruling class over darker and less talented peoples. As long as the Aryan masters remained racially pure, civilization continued to flourish. Unfortunately there was a strong tendency for the ruling minority to intermarry with, and ultimately to become indistinguishable from, the native population. Inevitably this was bound to result in the collapse of civilization. The only possible way of arresting this process of decay would be for the still-surviving Aryans to resist the temptations of miscegenation, and set to work producing a pure-bred ruling class for the benefit of future generations.

Anti-Semitism

A second and originally quite independent source of the Nazi ideology was anti-Semitism. During the long centuries of Christian faith, hostility to the Jews had always been a minor but persistent feature of Western civilization. Although early liberalism, with its emphasis on equal rights for all, had freed the Jews of their legal disabilities and recognized them as full citizens, much of the old hostility remained. Conservatives, in particular, were often disposed to resist all new-fangled claims to political and social equality, and to attribute many of the less acceptable features of modern life, including capitalism, to the rise of Jewish influence. As the power of Christianity waned, moreover, there was a growing tendency to interpret "the Jewish question" in racial rather than in strictly religious terms. Jews were resented not only as believers in an alien religion, but as members of an alien race. Extreme anti-Semites even went so far as to describe the whole course of modern history as the consequence of a malign Jewish conspiracy. Jewish capitalists and Jewish socialists, so the theory went, were united under the leadership of a secret committee known as the Elders of Zion, in a well-planned effort, diabolical in its cunning and worldwide in scope, to pull down the established order and to set up the Jewish people as masters and exploiters of the rest of the human race. By the time of World War I, this radical version of anti-Semitism, though generally confined to the lunatic fringe, was already a force to be reckoned with.

The "race science" of the Nazis managed to combine these various and rather unpromising elements in a single ideological system. Hitler was a poor and meagerly educated Austrian provincial who, as an unsuccessfully aspiring young artist, had gone to seek his fortune in Vienna. The Vienna of those prewar days was a teeming cosmopolitan city, the capital of a crumbling empire in which a beleaguered German minority was struggling, against increasingly hopeless odds, to retain control over a disaffected majority of non-Germanic peoples. In this hectic and unwholesome atmosphere, anti-Semitism and pan-Germanism were rife. Hitler absorbed these ideas, and developed an ineradicable belief in Germans as a master race engaged in a struggle to the death with tricky and resourceful racial inferiors. Feeling that Germany alone was strong enough to defend the interests of his race, he enlisted in the German army at the outbreak of World War I. The bitterness of seeing Germany meet defeat at the hands of a miscellaneous collection of alien peoples reinforced his earlier convictions. Confident that he himself was the person called by historic destiny to restore the master race to its rightful place in the world, he set to work building the Nazi party as a means to the attainment of that end. The ideology that inspired him, and by which he hoped to inspire others, was set forth in *Mein Kampf*, the passionate and disorderly book that he wrote to serve as the bible of the Nazi movement.

The Ideology of Nazism

Nazism was, in many ways, a typical modern ideology. As usual, it held forth the promise of a future kingdom of heaven on earth. The promised kingdom differed drastically from its liberal and socialist predecessors, however, in that it offered no hope of a society based on human equality and the minimization of political power. The new order was to be a permanent totalitarian dictatorship in which the master race fulfilled its natural and rightful function by exercising absolute and uncompromising rule over the inferior races of mankind. The Nazi movement did not, as its name might lead one to expect, conceive of this new order in strictly nationalist terms. Unlike fascism, which generally looked forward to the aggrandizement of a single nation-state, it conceived of the master race as a pure-bred racial elite whose members would be recruited not only from Germany but also from other countries, such as Great Britain, the United States, and the Scandinavian kingdoms, where Aryans and, above all, blond and blue-eyed Nordics, were especially plentiful. If these gifted people, riding roughshod over the principle of national self-determination and other so-called "human" rights, would only unite for the common purpose of conquering the rest of the world, the cause of civilization would be secure for at least a thousand years.

But if the master race was so supremely qualified to rule, how did it happen that it was not already in command? Nazism, as a proper ideology, had a ready answer to this question. Just as liberals and socialists had identified tyrants and capitalists, respectively, as the decisive obstacles to progress, the Nazis pointed to the Jews as the source of all evil. Of all the inferior races of mankind, the Semites were, by all odds, the most pernicious, since they too were, in their own diabolical way, a peculiarly gifted people. As parasites battening on the life-blood of alien societies, they had developed great skill in sapping the creative energies of the people among whom they lived. World Jewry was nothing less than a concerted plot to corrupt and destroy the master race. The Communist party, Wall Street, and the Vatican were but three of the many apparently disparate agencies they secretly controlled and used for the accomplishment of their purposes. Parliamentary democracy, with matchless resources of chaos and confusion, was one of their favorite devices. Honest Nordics were too innocent and simple-hearted to understand and offer resistance to such devious machinations. The result was progressive enslavement and corruption of the master race which thereby was increasingly disabled for the performance of its rightful functions.

The Cult of Leadership

What, then, was to be done? From the standpoint of Nazism this was an uncommonly difficult question. Unlike its predecessors, the Nazi ideology had no doctrine of historic necessity to offer as a stimulus to revolutionary action. The racist view of history was essentially regressive rather than progressive in character. Instead of growing from strength to strength, the position of the master race had clearly deteriorated in the past and there was no guarantee that it might not grow still weaker in the future. Lacking all faith in the inevitability of human progress, Nazism stood poles apart from the easily confident optimism of earlier ideologies.

To compensate for this weakness, the Nazis placed unprecedented stress on will and leadership. The theory of Italian fascism amounted to little more than faith in the Duce. "Mussolini is always right" was one of its typical slogans. The Führer occupied a similar place in the Nazi movement. Belief in the personal genius of Hitler was the central tenet of the Nazi political faith. He was the indispensable leader, the one and only superman who, by a supreme and inexplicable act of creative energy, could reverse the course of history and revive the master race. Since the days of primitive magic, the mystic cult of leadership has rarely been carried to greater heights.

The Limitations of Nazism

Considered as a whole, Nazi racism is by far the least impressive of the flights of modern ideology. Its intellectual underpinnings are flimsy, its range of interests narrow. With its appeal to an exclusive master race, it was bound to seem hateful to most people; and even among those to whom it was addressed there were many who could not stomach its ruthless disregard for all conventional moralities. Military victory was its only hope, and that hope proved unattainable. Moreover, because of its reliance on the genius of a single, unique individual, it had no genuine principle of political continuity. Thus the defeat and death of Hitler were followed by an immediate disintegration of the movement.

All this should not blind us to the fact, that while it lasted the Nazi movement was a tremendous political force. Although Hitler was less fortunate than Mussolini in his first bid for power, his ultimate success was far greater. In the political crisis that accompanied the unparalleled economic depression of the late 'twenties, the Nazi party grew with fantastic speed. By 1932 it had become the largest of all the German parties, commanding the support of no less than 40 per cent of the electorate. Hitler's appointment to the chancellorship in the following year was followed, much more surely and swiftly than in the case of Italy, by the establishment of a thoroughgoing totalitarian dictatorship. This paved the way for a series of diplomatic and military aggressions that had led, by 1943, to the conquest of most of Europe. Though the Nazi new order did not last long enough to develop its full potential, its revolutionary implications were amply demonstrated. Many millions of people were deliberately exterminated, many more millions enslaved and brutalized, in faithful accordance with the dictates of Nazi "race science." Short as it was, the Nazi experiment succeeded in shaking the deepest foundations of Western civilization. The power of ideology has never been more frightfully displayed.

CHAPTER TWELVE

TOWARDS 2000 A.D.: THE FUTURE OF IDEOLOGY

We have traced modern ideologies from the daydreams and fantasies of eighteenth-century liberals to the nightmare visions of twentieth-century fascists. The time has come, now, to pause and take stock of the situation. Have ideological ways of thought increased or decreased as a factor in politics since World War II? What role will ideology play in this, the last quarter of the twentieth century? These are the questions with which we shall concern ourselves in the course of this final chapter.

THE DECLINE OF IDEOLOGY IN WESTERN EUROPE

In the 1950s and early 1960s it seemed clear to all that ideological forces were waning. We have already seen how, by the end of World War I, the decline of revolutionary extremism had gone so far as to make it possible for liberals, socialists, and centrists to unite in support of the Weimar Republic. Although this trend toward an effective democratic consensus was for a time reversed by the Nazi and fascist movements, it was resumed even more strongly after World War II. In all the more advanced industrial countries of Western Europe, political life seemed to be dominated by parties firmly committed to the cause of constitutional democracy. Prosperity appeared to have been achieved under mixed economies, partly liberal and partly socialist in character, in which recognition of the advantages of free enterprise was combined with acceptance of the government's responsibility for a substantial range of social-service measures. Although some liberals continued to denounce this as "creeping socialism," and some Marxists still regarded it as a betrayal of working class interests, their voices for the moment seemed comparatively muted. In some of the larger and more influential socialist parties, most notably the British Labourites and the German Social Democrats, there were even official attempts to make a complete break with earlier ideological commitments, and to recognize that the nationalization of all industry was not the simple panacea it once was thought to be. Decreasing susceptibility to ideological extremism, and increasing willingness to negotiate within the framework of constitutional democracy, seemed to be the order of the day.

In the movement toward political consensus in postwar Europe, the rise of Christian democracy has played an important part, most notably in Germany and Italy and, to a lesser extent, in France. Although the Center party, in the aftermath of World War I, had been a leading participant in the Weimar coalition, it had never stood as a general voice for the supporters of conservative traditionalism. Large numbers of Christian traditionalists first adhered to the German nationalists, whose attitude toward the Weimar Republic was largely hostile, and subsequently switched to national socialism. This latter development was aided, for a time, by the Catholic Church itself. Pope Pius XI, whose encyclicals often spoke out against the sins of liberalism and socialism, made serious efforts to conciliate the Nazi and fascist regimes. By the end of World War II, however, the situation was quite different. The hopelessly anti-Christian and antitraditionalist character of the Nazi and fascist movements had by then been fully demonstrated, and the spread of communism to Eastern Europe caused great concern for the Church. Under Pius XII the church rallied strongly to the cause of constitutional democracy. Christian democratic parties arose to play a leading part in the political reconstruction of postwar Europe. An overwhelming majority of conservatives gave their allegiance to these parties. All this seemed to contribute to the healing of old ideological conflicts.

Also worthy of mention in this connection is the decline of militant nationalism. In earlier periods, the Mazzinian ideal of international cooperation had always been more promise than reality. Irreconcilable rivalries embittered the relationships between many European countries and heightened the tensions of domestic politics. Although it would be absurd to say that such rivalries ceased to exist, they certainly seemed much reduced in the postwar Western world. The unprecedented reconciliation of France and Germany, and the amazingly rapid progress of the Common Market, have brought the leading countries of Western Europe far closer than they ever were before. The movement toward European unity is by no means irreversible, but the nations of Western Europe have managed to go much farther than ever before toward the moderation of nationalist conflicts.

THE UNITED STATES AND THE SOVIET UNION

Ideological conflict seemed on the wane in the United States, as well, in the 1950s and early 1960s. Voting studies and public opinion polls repeatedly showed that the electorate seldom distinguished among candidates or parties on ideological or even policy lines. Extremist orientations appeared thoroughly uncongenial to an American public seemingly solidly locked into a moderate liberal consensus that eschewed alternatives of the right or left. Politics, in fact, proved uninteresting to the apathetic electorate, further evidence that Americans shared the general aversion to ideology that seemed to have permanently set in on the Western world.

Evidence for this general decline of ideology seemed even to be provided by the Marxist regime in the Soviet Union. Khrushchev's dramatic denunciation of Stalin in 1956 opened the door for what would emerge later as a full blown effort at peaceful coexistence with the West. Observers of Soviet society produced study upon study pointing to the moderation of the Marxist system in Russia and its general decline in fervor. Internal changes were discerned that seemed to suggest a general convergence of the Western and Soviet systems. Gradual changes were taking place in the camps of the antagonists, it was argued, which were making them more alike than dissimilar. The Chinese Communists, of course, agreed with this general reading of developments in the West and the Soviet Union.

Stability and order, moderation and calm, were the new principles of politics by the early 1960s. Ideological fervor and extremism were forever suspect as inappropriate and dangerous in a postwar world of compromise, consensus, and general prosperity.

THE REVIVAL OF IDEOLOGY

Most of these assumptions about a new nonideological age were destroyed in the decade between 1965 and 1975. These were years that saw the political and intellectual calm of the United States, Western Europe, and most of the world shattered by students, women, trade unionists, racial, ethnic and cultural minorities, intellectual dissidents, and cultural dropouts. What has emerged is a revival and reassertion of ideological politics on the grand scale. In all corners of the political world there are renewed and vigorous ideological perspectives at work.

It is now abundantly clear that the Age of Ideology was never really dead. It may well have abated for a short time after World War II, but even that was deceptive. The great ideologies of the last two hundred years continued even in that quiet period. While they persisted and even underwent rearticulation to ever stronger positions, totally new ideologies have emerged. The last quarter of the twentieth century has before it a dazzling array of ideological visions. A survey of these current ideologies is a fitting conclusion for this book. We began with the Age of Ideology, ushered in by one ideology—liberalism. We end now with a long list of ideologies.

Revisionist Liberalism

The most venerable ideology of the West has been very much on the defensive in the twentieth century, especially in intellectual circles. Buffeted for decades by criticism on its left and right, liberalism has experienced, however, a strong revival in recent years. Its economic ideals of a free market and governmental noninvolvement in the economy have persisted, and writers like Milton Friedman are in a continuous line that flows back to Adam Smith. There is little new on this score. What is new and capturing a good deal of attention, however, is a recent aggressive philosophical restatement of liberalism by the American philosopher, John Rawls.

In his *A Theory of Justice* Rawls has provided a most stimulating reworking of the liberal ideology. Its central premise is the inviolability of each and every individual which is to be maintained even in the face of claims of society's welfare. These just rights of individuals, Rawls contends, are immune from any form of social bargaining or any calculation of social interests. Rawls's argument is a profound updating of the traditional natural rights and social contract basis of liberal thought. He contends that a polity is just when all persons have an equal right to the most extensive liberty which is compatible with a like liberty for all. Inequalities will be tolerated only if they work to everyone's advantage, especially society's least advantaged, and assuming that the position or office to which they are attached or from which they may be gained are open to all. It is the liberal's powerful commitment to equality of opportunity restated and refined. Rawls calls this principle fair opportunity. The family and social origins of individuals must be equalized, too, if this is to be real equality of opportunity. These liberal principles are just and fair, according to Rawls, because they are such as any free and rational person would have accepted in some hypothetical position of equality, the state of nature in Locke's social contract argument, when no one knew their ultimate place in society, their abilities or wealth.

The widespread excitement generated by Rawls's book is due in no small part to its self-conscious restatement of liberal fundamentals. It is done, to be sure, with a heavy dose of democratic egalitarianism. Indeed, some of his conservative critics have attacked Rawls as a twentieth-century Rousseau. This overlooks, however, Rawls's oft-repeated insistence on ranking individual liberty above equality as a social priority in a just society. This just society, while calling for equal liberty and fair opportunity still tolerates the existence of class and individual inequality. Rawls does envision a governmental role in the economy that would modify the free competitive market in order to maintain decent minimum standards of living. But this governmental intervention is intended only to prevent concentrations of power and to promote a truly fair equality of opportunity. The ruling economic principles are those of the free market and the political theory is liberal. In Rawls's writings, the liberalism of Locke, Smith, and Paine has found a powerful and articulate new voice.

New Conservatism

Recent years have seen a dramatic revival of Burkean conservatism, especially in the United States. Beginning in the late 1960s, an influential group of new conservatives has emerged here, that includes among its spokesmen Nathan Glazer, Irving Kristol, Daniel Patrick Moynihan, James Q. Wilson, and Edward Banfield. Most of these conservative thinkers are academics and journalists. Many were formerly liberals or radicals who have moved right in reaction to the militant ideological politics of blacks, students, and war protesters in the 1960s. Others have come to conservatism after disillusionment with the Great Society's efforts to eliminate poverty and prejudice from the American scene.

The themes developed by the conservatives all echo those originally articulated by Burke. Society is complex, they insist, and there are no simple solutions to its problems. Liberals and radicals are accused of causing more harm by their efforts to remake society than existed in the evil they react against. The decline of religious faith and the ascendency of intellectuals and social scientists is lamented. Human beings, it is held, live in a flawed world where perfection is an illusory goal and where suffering and injustice are givens of the human condition. Like Burke, the new conservatives reject the utopianism of liberal ideology and the radical commitment to the attainment of equality and freedom. Liberals and radicals, they insist, are engaged in a foolish and tragic rejection of all those features of tradition, excellence, authority, and inherited values that make our less than perfect humanity at least tolerable. Nearly two hundred years ago, Burke had said that that was the most one could hope for.

Anti-Colonialism

In many parts of the post-war world, far from there having been any decline there has been an explosive growth in ideological fervor. Colonial governments everywhere in Asia and Africa have been supplanted or threatened by anticolonial movements based on the old revolutionary principle of national self-determination. For much of this Third World the latter half of the twentieth century seems in fact but the beginning of the Age of Ideology. Modern ideologies first arose in the Western world, after all, as an accompaniment of the Industrial Revolution. They developed in a period of radical readjustment, when old-established habits of thought and action were being forced to make way for an unprecedentedly rapid series of economic and political developments. This is exactly the case today in most of the Third World.

The ideologies fueling the anticolonial movement have been in many cases updated versions of the venerable ideologies of the West. Most of the African, Asian, and South American nationalist leaders had studied in the United States, Europe, or the Soviet Union. They were schooled in the liberal principles of natural rights and self-determination; or the democratic ideas of equality and fraternity; or the Marxist vision of social justice. Many of them were deeply influenced by Marxist–Leninist writings on imperialism. But these ideological movements were not total imports. Often the ideology of the West was blended with or even subordinated to more native ideological visions. Pan-Arabism and Pan-Africanism have been one set of trans-national alternatives, and Arab socialism, African socialism, or Latin American corporatism another national set. Despite their wide divergence, what is common to all these alternatives is some claim to much older and more deeply rooted local traditions and ideals as inspiration for today's ideological movements.

The ideology of anticolonialism persists even after the imperial powers have been ousted, and even in Third World areas with long traditions of nationhood and self-government. What explains this apparent paradox is the continued and often increased economic presence and domination by the foreigner long after the overt political presence and domination have ended, or even when it never existed. This neocolonialism leaves many Third World nations with their economy very much at the mercy of foreign investors from the great multi-national corporations based in the industrialized world. The Marxist writings on the imperialist imperatives of world capitalism are particularly appealing, then, to the anticolonialist movement today. They seem to be an all too accurate description of their everyday reality. Here, too, is evidence of the amazing continuities in the Age of Ideology.

Neo-Marxism

From its apparent lack of influence during the 1950s and 1960s, Marxism both as a political movement and intellectual force has experienced a dramatic renaissance in Western Europe during the 1970s. The Communist parties of Italy, France, and now Spain and Portugal have virtually broken with Moscow, culminating a process that began with the rupture over the Soviet invasion of Hungary. These parties are now powerful players in the democratic politics of these Latin countries. Their doctrine of Eurocommunism commits them to participation in nonrevolutionary electoral and parliamentary politics. The crucial development has been the break with Moscow and the commitment to a native European communist ideal. This ideal sees neither seeking national solutions nor collaboration with bourgeois parties and processes as incompatible with Marxist ideological goals.

Parallel to its political resurgence, Marxism has also experienced in recent years a dramatic intellectual rebirth. The efforts of the Frankfurt School to combine Marx, Hegel, and Freud have had a profound impact on intellectual circles of Europe and America, especially through the writings of its most well known member, Herbert Marcuse. But probably the most influential neo-Marxist writings today are those of the late Italian Marxist, Antonio Gramsci. In his *Prison Notebooks* Gramsci offered the theory of "hegemony," a provocative explanation for the continued success of Western capitalism in resisting proletarian revolution. In capitalist society, he wrote, the dominant economic class exercises sheer coercive force through the state and governmental apparatus, to be sure. But this alone cannot explain its incredible and perpetual control over society. Matching the role of coercive force in the political realm is the dominant class's hegemony in the social, cultural, and moral realm. The ideology of the ruling class, its interests and needs, permeates the masses of the population and all their attitudes and institutions. In other words, without using the coercive apparatus of the state the ruling class keeps and justifies its dominance through the active consent of those over whom it rules. The public is educated to give this consent by schools, churches, and intellectuals who work for the ruling class.

Gramsci's is a revision of Marx that has impressed many. The ruling class in capitalist society rules not only by force, he insists, but also through the consent of the ruled, to the extent that the latter are culturally and intellectually convinced that the ruling class should rule. The weapon of force, the state, is really only a reserve power needed for moments of crisis when spontaneous hegemonic consent has failed in capitalist society. Gramsci's neo-Marxist theories help explain the incredible resiliency of bourgeois civilization, while at the same time offering a new set of revolutionary tactics to its opponents. The state, and thus the power of the ruling class, in advanced capitalist societies is protected by a whole set of hegemonic relationships within the society. Revolutionary strategy dedicated on the Russian model to the immediate seizure of the state apparatus is thus folly. It would destroy only one aspect of ruling-class power, leaving its general hegemony untouched.

Marxist revolutionaries, Gramsci suggests, if they are to be successful, must first undermine the hegemony of bourgeois values and beliefs for the ruled classes, before they seek political takeovers. This task he assigns to the Communist party, which will educate the proletariat in a "counterhegemony," based on the ideal of proletariat homogeneity and consciousness. The proletariat will receive from the party a new and higher conception of the world. They will come to live and believe a counter ideology. Faith in these new intellectual and moral ideals must precede political revolution. Only then, according to Gramsci, will seizure of the bourgeois state be worthwhile and meaningful.

Maoism

The Chinese Revolution must be added to the series of revolutions that have formed the political foundation on which the Age of Ideology has been built. This cataclysmic upheaval in the lives of so many hundreds of millions involved much more than the fall of Chiang Kai-shek and the nationalist government in 1949, however. In the course of three decades, while in power, and for many years while coming to power, the Chinese revolutionaries have transformed one of the world's poorest and most backward nations into a modern industrial giant. The principal architect of this achievement was Mao Tse-tung. As the success of China has become the model dazzling many of the impoverished and exploited nations in today's Third World, so the ideology of Mao has become a principal source of revolutionary inspiration.

Maoism means many things, but at least three features stand out. More than anything else it is committed to the central role of the peasantry in social revolution, and in carrying the revolutionary struggle, based on peasant grievances, from the countryside to the towns. This involved an even more fundamental departure from Marx than Lenin had made. Still, Mao saw this "new democratic" revolution based on peasant power as within the Marxist-Leninist theory of permanent revolution. Like Lenin, Mao also wrote often of the need to adapt decisively and creatively to the social realities of a given revolutionary situation—in this case, the huge peasant population and the accumulated centuries of peasant misery in all colonial and semicolonial peoples.

The second critical feature of Maoism is its conviction that revolutionary struggle is indeed the struggle of revolutionary armies. Mao's great strategic innovation was the use of long protracted war as both a vehicle to mobilize the masses and to overthrow the enemies of the masses. Revolutionary war was not conventional warfare. A people's war against its oppressors took the form of guerrilla warfare. Mao clearly spelled out the basic tactics of guerrilla warfare:

> "The enemy advances, we retreat; the enemy camps, we harass; the enemy tires, we attack; the enemy retreats, we pursue."

In the base areas everyone joined the fighting—troops and civilians, men and women, old and young. In the course of battle a revolutionary consciousness was formed, rendered articulate by the leadership of the party.

A final feature of Maoism worth singling out is its aggressive antibureaucratic bias. Mao was obsessed that no moderating party or state apparatus set itself up between the masses and the constant quest for revolutionary objectives. This concept of "the mass line," the direct link between the masses and the revolutionary leadership, made Mao suspicious of party functionaries with vested bureaucratic interests. The revolution was a permanent one, never ending. The zeal for revolutionary transformation never rested. Constant renewal of revolutionary fervor was required, constant returns to the mass base of the movement were necessary. Respectable and responsible party or state administrators, comfortably presiding over a routine and rational post-revolutionary order, as in the Soviet Union, are images repugnant to the Maoist ideological vision. Perpetual revolutionary passion and involvement, constant retouching of the popular base—these are the demands made by contemporary Maoism.

Anarchism

Recent years have seen a resurgence of interest in anarchism, an ideology whose origins are in the eighteenth and nineteenth centuries. Anarchists then and now sense what they take to be the paradox at the heart of the liberal ideal of the state. On the one hand, liberalism presumes a naturally harmonious society and views government and the state with suspicion. It therefore stresses limits and restraints on the authority of the state. On the other hand, liberalism recognizes state coercion, when voluntarily agreed to by individuals seeking to protect their natural rights, as the only legitimate source of coercion. Liberals, according to anarchists, despite their antistate bias, offer a profound justification of the modern state.

It is this modern coercive state that anarchists repudiate. They would replace it with noncoercive alternatives. But, while they agree in their opposition to the centralized state, anarchists are far from united on what should replace that state as the ideal social order. While they may agree that the alternative should in some way involve decentralized and local political units, they split seriously when turning to specifics. Their disagreement has produced two main tendencies within the anarchist camp, two tendencies which developed in the nineteenth century and which flourish today in the contemporary revival of anarchism.

One important strain of anarchism is individualist in emphasis. It envisions a restructured social order in which the centralized authoritarian state has been replaced with a social order peopled by autonomous and independent individuals totally free from any form of social or political control or force. Central to this individuality and freedom for many anarchists in this camp has been the institution of private property which serves as a crucial bulwark insuring the autonomy and independence of individuals.

The theorists of individualist anarchism would include the English philosopher William Godwin (1756–1836) and, in the nineteenth century, Americans like Henry David Thoreau and Benjamin Tucker. In recent years a libertarian school has emerged in America that is a vocal ideological expression of this individualist anarchist tradition. Its spokesmen (Murray Rothbard is a leading example) call for the dismantling of centralized government and the replacement of its functions by private, voluntary, and contractual bodies. All government services, according to these libertarian anarchists, can be performed by private agencies. Rothbard would include even police, judicial, and defense functions. Only through such voluntary and contractual arrangements can individuals be free, Rothbard insists.

Another important tendency in anarchist ideology is a communalist tradition which would replace the centralized state not with atomistic independent individuals but with cooperative communal groups characterized by social solidarity and mutual aid. The emphasis is not on individuality and autonomy but on community, on cooperation, and sharing. More often than not communal anarchists have repudiated private property, and their ideology has thus been closer to the Marxist tradition, just as individualist anarchists have been closer to the liberal tradition. Theorists of communal anarchism include the great nineteenth-century antagonists of Marx, Bakunin and Kropotkin. Both broke from Marxism because they felt it would perpetuate the power of the centralized state in the guise of proletariat domination.

Communal anarchism has experienced a significant revival in recent years. A strong component of the counterculture of the 1960s was resurgence of both urban and rural communes organized on anarchist principles of non-authoritarian, non-hierarchical sharing and cooperation. Intellectuals like Murray Bookchin have argued that advances of technology make possible now the decentralization of both the state and the economy. The complexity of the centralized state, he argues, is artificial and contrived. He envisions a new order of small local communities, self-contained and self-governing. Free communities, free sharing and cooperative communities, would replace the centralized bureaucratic state.

Feminism

The final ideological movement to emerge in the 1970s is feminism. As an ideology it, too, has roots deep in the eighteenth and nineteenth century. Mary Wollstonecraft's *Vindication of the Rights of Woman*, written in 1793, was part of the broader liberal movement in that it argued persuasively for the extension of legal, political, and educational equality to women. John Stuart Mill in the next century urged, still within the liberal tradition, the reform of marriage laws, woman's suffrage, and most important, extension of equal opportunity to women of talent and merit. Marxist writers of the nineteenth century were keenly interested in the relationship between men and women. They saw the family as the generic source of the division of labor and the relationship of wife and child to the husband as the prototypical source of notions of dominance and private property. Within the family the man, Marxists wrote, was the bourgeois and the wife the proletariat. The equality of women would be achieved, Marxists contended, with the end of exploitation by capital and the transference of private housework to public industry.

By the late 1960s it was becoming clear to many women, however, that neither liberal nor Marxist ideology, nor the alleged advances resulting from the suffragette movement, had done much if anything to end the subordinate role that Western culture, secular and religious, had given them. It was in the context of this realization that there emerged in the midst of the general revival of ideological activity in the late 1960s and early 1970s a new and militant feminism. Three broad strains can be discerned within the movement.

The first is merely a more militant incarnation of the older ideology of liberal feminism. Its concerns are absolute equality of opportunity, the elimination of all sexual differentials. Equal pay for equal work, abortion reform, and the Equal Rights Amendment make up the cornerstone of its program. This militant liberalism is by far the most popular variety of feminism today, but it is being challenged intellectually by two other tendencies within the movement.

Radical feminists, like Shulamith Firestone, contend that mere liberal reform of existing society will never reach or modify the root cause of woman's oppression. Economic power and economic change are also tangential to what is crucial-sexual oppression. History is the tale of male oppression, of patriarchal power, not of economic or class power. Woman is oppressed as a given of biological reality. Her reproductive function and her role in the biological family are at the heart of her secondary position. The sexual, not the economic, division of labor is where Firestone finds the root problem. What must be done is to repudiate totally the sexual division of labor, to restructure and ultimately do away with the traditional nuclear family. For some radical feminists the solution is lesbianism—the creation of an autonomous and independent feminine existence, free of the oppressive agent, man.

A third strand within the feminist movement, the socialist feminists, is represented by writers like the Englishwoman, Sheila Rowbotham. As their name implies, their concern is to forge a synthesis between the class analysis of Marxists and the patriarchal analysis of the radical feminists. The subordinate role of women today, they contend, is derived both from the timeless laws of biology with their oppression by patriarchal males, as well as the historical laws of economic development and the exploitation by male capitalists. The solution for socialist feminists is a movement that moves on two fronts: replacing the received notion of the sexual division of labor and the nuclear family, while also replacing the capitalist economy with a socialist, nonalienated classless society.

THE FUTURE

Some of today's ideologies contemplate great transformations in the existing social and political order. Others argue for the continuation of that order and insist that the existing relationships between classes or sexes is appropriate and just. They run the gamut from the new conservatism's anti-ideological plea for what is, to the socialist feminists' demand for a true equality between men and women that would render obsolete virtually all of existing society's institutions and patterns of life. The choice for some is what variety and what degree of perfection they seek, and what price they are willing to pay for it. For many others the search for perfection is itself illusory and the proper quest is the more practical one of compromise and stability.

Ideologies, we said at the outset of this book, have usually sought utopias on earth, total transformations and improvements of the flawed world that exists. Ideologies seek to turn the world upside down, to make it over so that the new world is utterly at variance with what went before. The partisans of an ideology think the new order is good, their opponents think the world ought not be turned around. What is constant, however, is that ideologies do seek to topple old ways. The last ideology we have looked at, feminism, would no doubt change the world considerably, but so did the very first we looked at, the liberalism of the American Revolution. It would do well to remember that in 1781, as Cornwallis surrendered to Washington at Yorktown, he ordered melancholy tunes played by his band, according to the military etiquette of the day. Among them he asked that one particular old English nursery rhyme be played:

> If buttercups buzz
> after the bee;
> If boats were on land
> churches on sea;
> If ponies rode men,
> and grass ate the cow;
> If cats should be chased
> into holes by the mouse;

If mammas sold their babies
to gypsies for half a crown;
If summer were spring
and the other way round
Then all the world would be upside down.

That the Americans had defeated the English, that the child had rejected the parent, was violation of all that seemed natural; that simple, egalitarian Americans had defeated the defenders of privilege and rank was the world turned upside down for Cornwallis.

Today's ideologists are, for better or for worse, not unlike these earlier liberal American revolutionaries. They, too, seek dramatic ruptures and new beginnings. Like Tom Paine, with whom we began, they think ideologically. He, of course, lived to see the realization of his utopia. Writing to a Frenchman about the American Revolution he noted:

> Our style and manner of thinking have undergone a revolution. We see with other eyes; we hear with other ears; and we think with other thoughts, than those we formerly used."

Whether some of us will, whether we want to, whether we ought to, is another matter.

TO EXPLORE FURTHER

The most obvious, and probably the best way to embark on further study of the subject is to read as many as possible of the original writings on which this book is based. In this day of inexpensive paperback editions, most of the original writings are now readily available, and there is no reason why a selection of these should not be used. Some suitable titles are the following: Thomas Paine, *Common Sense* (New York: Viking-Penguin, 1977): John Locke, *Treatise of Civil Government* (New York: Appleton-Century-Croft, 1937); Adam Smith, *The Wealth of Nations* (New York: Viking-Penguin, 1970); Jean Jacques Rousseau, *On the Social Contract* (New York: St. Martin's, 1977); Edmund Burke, *Reflexions on the Revolution in France* (New York: The Liberal Arts Press, 1955); Joseph Mazzini, *The Duties of Man and Other Essays* (New York: Dutton, 1936); John Stuart Mill, *On Liberty* (New York: The Liberal Arts Press, 1956); Karl Marx, *Selected Writings* (Oxford: Oxford University Press, 1977); Gerard F. Yates, S. J., *Papal Thought on the State: Excerpts from Encyclicals and Other Writings of Recent Popes* (New York: Appleton-Century-Crofts, 1958); Eduard Bernstein, *Evolutionary Socialism* (New York: Schocken Books, 1961); V. I. Lenin, *What Is To Be Done* (New York: International Publishers, 1929); Adolf Hitler, *Mein Kampf* (Boston: Houghton Mifflin, 1962). Other important works, by the same authors and others, are also readily available, but these suggestions for further reading will serve as a starting point.

In the last chapter numerous examples of contemporary ideological writings are surveyed. Further reading on this score would include: John Rawls, *A Theory of Justice* (Cambridge: Harvard University Press, 1971); Franz Fanon, *The Wretched of the Earth* (New York: Grove Press, 1965); Daniel Guerin, *Anarchism* (New York: Monthly Review Books, 1970); Antonio Gramsci, *Antonio Gramsci: Selections From His Political Writings* (New York: International Publishing Co., 1977); Stuart Schram, *The Political Thought of Mao Tse-Tung* (New York: Praeger, 1969); Sheila Rowbotham, *Woman's Consciousness, Man's World* (London: Penguin, 1973); Zillah Eisenstein, *Capitalist Patriarchy and the Case for Socialist Feminism* (New York: Monthly Review Press, 1978).

So much for the primary sources. Turning now to secondary materials, it is possible to mention only a few of the many works in which the themes suggested in this book could be pursued with profit. On the concept of ideology itself, and its relationship to political theory, the classic work is Karl Mannheim, *Ideology and Utopia: An Introduction to the Sociology of Knowledge* (New York: Harcourt, Brace, 1936), a work too difficult, perhaps, to be recommended to beginners. More recent works on ideology include: John Plamenatz, *Ideology* (London: Macmillan, 1970); George Lichtheim, *The Concept of Ideology* (New York: Vintage Books, 1967); M. Rejai (ed.), *Decline of Ideology?* (Chicago: Aldine/Atherton, 1971).

There have also been a number of interesting attempts to develop a general theory of modern revolutions, including the ideological aspects. Among these are Hannah Arendt, *On Revolution* (New York: Viking, 1963); Crane Brinton, *The Anatomy of Revolution* (Englewood Cliffs, N.J.: Prentice-Hall, 1952); Jacob L. Talmon, *The Rise of Totalitarian Democracy* (Boston: The Beacon Press, 1952); Chalmers Johnson, *Revolutionary Change* (Boston: Little, Brown, 1966); Barbara Salert, *Revolutions and Revolutionaries* (New York: Elsevier, 1976); A. S. Cohan, *Theories of Revolution* (New York: Wiley, 1975).

There are also a number of books which deal with the problems of the Age of Ideology as a part of the general history of the West and of western political thought. The most comprehensive of these are George H. Sabine, *A History of Political Theory* (New York: Holt, Rinehart and Winston, 1961); and, more recently, Sheldon Wolin, *Politics and Vision* (Boston: Little, Brown, 1960). More historical in orientation are: Eric Hobsbawn, *The Age of Revolution* (New York: Mentor, 1973); Mulford Q. Sibley, *Political Ideas and Ideologies* (New York: Harper & Row, 1970); Robert Palmer, *The Age of the Democratic Revolution* (Princeton: Princeton University Press, 1969); Barrington Moore, *Social Origins of Dictatorship and Democracy* (Boston: Beacon, 1966); E. P. Thompson, *The Making of the English Working Class* (New York: Vintage, 1963). Readers interested in knowing more about the authors' views on these matters might consult Frederick Watkins, *The Political Tradition of the West* (Cambridge: Harvard University Press, 1962) and Isaac Kramnick, *The Rage of Edmund Burke* (New York: Basic Books, 1977).

Finally, a few suggested readings on special topics. On early liberalism, in France and England respectively, see Carl L. Becker, *The Heavenly City of the Eighteenth-Century Philosophers* (New Haven: Yale University Press, 1932); and Elie Halévy, *The Growth of Philosophic Radicalism* (Boston: The Beacon Press, 1955). The standard work on the whole utilitarian movement, including J. S. Mill, is Leslie Stephen, *The English Utilitarians*, 3 vols. (London: London School of Economics and Political Science, 1950). For those who do not wish to face so long and ponderous a work, John Plamenatz, *The English Utilitarians* (Oxford: Oxford University Press, 1958) is recommended. Readers might also consult: Harold Laski, *The Rise of European Liberalism* (London: Allen Unwin, 1958); Alfred Cobban, *Aspects of the French Revolution* (Braziller, 1968); Bernard Bailyn, *The Ideological Origins of the American Revolution* (Cambridge: Harvard University Press, 1967). For the relationship of democratic and liberal theory see, C. B. MacPherson, *The Political Theory of Possessive Individualism* (Oxford: Oxford University Press, 1962) and *Democratic Theory* (Oxford: Oxford University Press, 1973).

On nationalism, the best introduction is to be found in two books by Hans Kohn, *The Idea of Nationalism* (New York: Macmillan, 1944) and *Prophets and Peoples* (New York: Macmillan, 1957). The latter includes a good chapter on Mazzini. Of the numberless books on Marxism and its derivatives, the following are especially useful: S. Avineri, *Karl Marx: Social and Political Thought* (Cambridge, Eng.: Cambridge University Press, 1968); David McLellan, *Karl Marx* (New York: Viking, 1975); Bertell Ollman, *Alienation: Marx's Conception of Man in Capitalist Society* (Cambridge: Cambridge University Press, 1971).

INDEX